The Joy of Teaching

The Joy of Teaching
Effective Strategies for the Classroom

HARRY HAZEL

◆PICKWICK *Publications* • Eugene, Oregon

THE JOY OF TEACHING
Effective Strategies for the Classroom

Copyright © 2010 Harry Hazel. All rights reserved. Except for brief quotations in critical publications or reviews, no part of this book may be reproduced in any manner without prior written permission from the publisher. Write: Permissions, Wipf and Stock Publishers, 199 W. 8th Ave., Suite 3, Eugene, OR 97401.

Pickwick Publications
An Imprint of Wipf and Stock Publishers
199 W. 8th Ave., Suite 3
Eugene, OR 97401

www.wipfandstock.com

ISBN 13: 978-1-60608-613-1

Cataloging-in-Publication data:

Hazel, Harry.

    The joy of teaching : effective strategies for the classroom / Harry Hazel.

    xii + 146 p. ; 23 cm. — Includes bibliographical references.

    ISBN 13: 978-1-60608-613-1

    1. Teaching. 2. Teacher effectiveness. I. Title.

LB1027 H386 2010

Manufactured in the U.S.A.

*This book is dedicated to my wife, Kathleen,
for her constant support and love.*

Contents

List of Illustrations • *viii*

Preface • *ix*

Acknowledgments • *xi*

1. Why Is Teaching So Rewarding? • 1
2. Motivating Yourself to Teach • 10
3. Motivating Students • 21
4. Tools to Teach: The Lecture, Discussion, Dialectic, Textbook, and Computers • 36
5. Polishing Speaking Skills • 53
6. How to Take the Pain out of Writing for Teachers and Students • 69
7. Organizing, Planning, and Time Management for the Teacher without Much Time • 80
8. Finding Joy Outside the Classroom • 91
9. Dealing with Problems as Challenges: Discipline, Grading, Plagiarism, and Difficult Colleagues • 99
10. Homework and Testing • 112
11. Humor and the Enjoyment of Teaching • 123
12. Making the Joy Last • 132

Bibliography • *143*

List of Illustrations

Figure 1   Balanced and Unbalanced Crosses • 8

Figure 2   Big Box, Little Box • 57

Preface

> "We tend to enjoy those things we do well."
> —Anonymous

When members of the media asked John F. Kennedy to describe happiness, he would often refer to the ancient Greeks' definition of happiness as the development of talents along lines of excellence. These principles epitomize the approach taken in this book. Not all teachers enjoy their profession, but for those who do, two reasons often stand out: they're excellent teachers and they get great satisfaction from their work, especially as it impacts students.

The twelve chapters present a number of approaches gleaned from over forty years in various classrooms. Three of those years were spent in teaching high school students. I taught in a community college for four more years. During graduate studies, I taught in two large universities. During the past thirty-eight years I taught in a liberal arts university.

I am well aware that this treatise is top-heavy on material from colleges and universities. I hope instructors from other grade levels gain some useful insights. I am also aware that readers will not agree with some of the approaches described in the book. Teachers have a wide variety of teaching skills that serve them well, many of which are not in this book. *Viva la difference!*

Acknowledgments

THE FOUR GONZAGA UNIVERSITY faculty and staff listed below were extremely helpful in offering technical and library assistance during the writing of this book. I am very grateful for the time they spent in applying their talents.

Kelly Jenks

Jason Gilman

Susan Millar

Janet Brougher

1

Why Is Teaching So Rewarding?

> If you want happiness for a day, go fishing
> If you want happiness for a year, inherit a fortune.
> If you want happiness for a lifetime, help someone else.
>
> —Chinese proverb

IN THE MOVIE *EDUCATING Rita,* Michael Caine plays an alcoholic professor who tutors a twenty-five-year-old British hairdresser. The main character, Rita, comes from a working-class background, and despite protestations from her laborer husband that "she ought to have babies" instead of going to school, Rita persists. In one poignant moment, Rita has just seen *Macbeth* and can't wait to share the experience with her mentor. She approaches his university building and sees him giving a lecture. Undismayed, she peeks in the window and taps on the glass. He comes to the door and listens while she excitedly tells about her reaction to Shakespeare's play. Instead of chiding her for interrupting the class, the professor tells Rita he's honored she would share this special moment with him.

The film is fictitious, but experiences like the one described are not. A few students who get excited about learning make up for the many others who believe the material is about as captivating as reading the Smith section of the New York phone book. Teaching is a joy for both teacher and students when the lights of learning go on and continue to glow.

Every teacher can spin tales of frustration about apathetic students, insensitive administrators and cantankerous colleagues. But such hassles go with the territory. Fulfilled professionals will cite ten positive experiences for every negative one and such experiences keep them in the classroom.

The Joy of Teaching

Arnold Patent was an attorney for twenty-five years and made a salary that allowed him to live the "good life." But it left him with ashes in his soul. He felt tired, frustrated, and tense. After consulting with a number of physicians, he knew he was stressed out and unfulfilled because he wasn't doing what he wanted. So he quit his practice and started giving workshops on his philosophy of life—a philosophy which, in a nutshell, advocates doing what you enjoy, rather than what you think you need to do. The "best life" is developing one's unique set of talents, especially in the service of others.

REWARDS OF TEACHING

One major reward of teaching is to find meaning in one's life. *Meaning* is an abstract term and can be applied in a number of ways. Meaning is fulfillment, self-actualization, and the knowledge that one's life makes a difference. Prisoners in camps were able to rise above their squalid conditions and face the future with hope. For some, meaning was the constant image of a loved one back home. For others, meaning was an unfinished product like a book or man. For still others, meaning was doing God's work as they saw it amid the pain of the camps.

Many a retired teacher can look back and reflect with deep pleasure on a life that meant something. Piling up wealth may bring some comfort and security, but it doesn't match the bone-deep satisfaction of knowing that one has developed her talents and has made numerous people better because she was there.

Rabbi Harold Kushner (*When All You've Ever Wanted Isn't Enough*) emphasizes that the key barometer of success is not fame or wealth, but the realization that one has made a difference. Kushner quotes his teacher Abraham Joshua Heschel, who used to tell him: "When I was young, I admired clever people. Now that I am old, I admire kind people." Meaning for Kushner is found in serving other people and developing one's own talents.

Kushner emphasized that even suffering can have meaning if it is endured for the right reason. If pain is simply endured, it has little or no value. But if suffering is part of loving someone or is experienced in doing something worthwhile, it can have enormous value. Most people will avoid pain if they can. But those same people will admit that anything worth accomplishing usually involves some pain. No teacher can avoid some suffering during a long career because the heartaches, ennui and stresses go with the job. But most of what educators term pain has a purpose. Interaction with difficult students, struggling with new courses and enduring the inevitable squabbles with others is part of education.

Not everyone is cut out to teach. We all have different gifts, and the key to happiness is to develop one's unique talents in an atmosphere of success. Some might like the prestige of being a doctor, but they don't excel in science and hate the sight of blood. The prestige would have to be strong to overcome a basic aversion to practicing medicine. Numerous teachers have started a career in education and discovered they're not suited to its demands. For them, teaching is far from fulfilling. Such people either get out as soon as they can or stay because they have to earn a salary but hate every minute of their ordeal. But those who like contact with people, who enjoy learning themselves, and who like to see students blossom will find unmatched fulfillment in their profession.

TEACHERS' REACTIONS TO WHAT MAKES TEACHING SATISFYING

In doing research for this book, I collected reactions from over one hundred teachers about why they like what they do. The vast majority focused on the students or "kids" and talked in terms of "touching lives" and "really making a difference." The teachers rarely mentioned salary or fringe benefits. Most emphasized the joy of helping students learn and seeing those students develop their potential.

We can have three effects on people: they can be worse because we were there, they can stay the same, or they can get better. Teaching offers one of the best chances of making them better.

Joyce Neubauer was a first-grade teacher for many years. She loves teaching, because she can "empower children to be the best they can be—to make their own unique contribution, to celebrate their lives." She believes strongly in Aristotle's principle that "the purpose of education is to develop our vital powers along lines of excellence." She also stresses the need to be child-centered and not subject matter-centered. For her, a teacher's job is not to impose a rigid, limited set of knowledge on six-year-olds but to maximize learning for each student during the time given for teaching. Joyce describes the rewards she receives: "The best part is that I learn from them how to celebrate the ordinary—something that adults do not seem to do well. It is both reinforcing and exhilarating to be around people for whom every picture painted, every new word learned is a celebration."

George Park decided in the fourth grade to be a teacher—a decision he's never regretted. He teaches in a middle school and explains the challenge of his work: "My biggest challenge is to turn the hearts of my students to being interested in their own futures and being excited about the possibilities on the horizon. And bringing energy into the classroom to make what happens here dynamic and interesting for my students. That was the biggest challenge of my first year of teaching it remains the same today." Carol Stumpf teaches high school and states that she finds joy in her profession because "I love sharing what I know, and I love learning myself. School is the perfect setting for both of these."

Rod Clefton worked in the broadcast industry for twenty-five years before he began a second career at a private university teaching courses in television and radio. With his rich baritone voice, Rod was in constant demand for radio and television work. He relished his hours with students and found immense satisfaction when he saw his graduates land media jobs across the United States. But for him, contact with teaching colleagues is a plus one doesn't always find in business. He says, "I like walking into the faculty lounge with nothing particular on my mind and being engaged by people from other disciplines on topics which range from politics to Plato."

Dave Darrant has taught primary students for seventeen years in Calgary, Alberta, and says that all but one of the seventeen has been fantastic. The enthusiasm of his students motivates him, but he also singles out the joy of learning: "Since becoming a teacher, I have learned more by teaching."

Most fulfilled teachers talk about touching the lives of their students. A troubled adolescent comes back twenty years after high school and says, "You really turned my life around. I thought just about everything you said and taught was crap back then, but you didn't give up on me. You finally showed me that learning not only opened doors in my profession, but also exposed me to the stimulating world of learning for the pure pleasure of it."

Why Is Teaching So Rewarding?

THE WORD *EDUCARE*

The Latin word *educare* means to "draw out." Most educators find that their main source of joy is to take students at one level of learning and then to advance them as far as possible during the time they're together in the classroom or lab. Like Joyce Neubauer, satisfied teachers focus on students. They teach people—not reading, speech or economics. They know their subject matter well, but students are their primary concern. Each class brings the challenge of new students who can be "drawn out" and nudged along on their journey to self-development. A first-grade teacher shows her charges how to read and gives them a tool they'll use forever. A high-school science instructor explains the intricacies of a subject that students have avoided and shows them how chemistry can give them a much better understanding of medicine. A community-college computer instructor takes adults who fear machines and points out how they can save hours in a busy schedule by using a word processor. Good teachers challenge, cajole, prod, push and move each student as far as they can.

Teachers "give away" knowledge. Lowman (*Mastering the Techniques of Teaching*) emphasizes that "Teaching students what one knows ... provides the warm satisfaction that comes whenever ones gives away something one values, as when one purchases a present or composes a poem for a special occasion." Lowman goes on to state that satisfied teachers are "compulsive sharers of what they know" (ibid). On the other hand, instructors who find little joy in giving to others find far less joy in what they do.

TEACHERS WHO MADE A DIFFERENCE

Anyone who loves teaching can look back at master teachers who made a difference and who inspired them to follow education as a life-long career. Some might remember a first-grade teacher—a strict nun with a heart of gold who gave a small religious statue on a day when no one else came to school because of a snowstorm. Others might recall a high school history instructor who made battles come alive with illustrations and imitations of famous historical characters.

For me, one such teacher was Dominic LaRusso. Sometimes referred to as "Dynamic Dominic," this college professor with the remnants of a New York accent epitomized the finest qualities in a first-rate teacher. He was a spellbinding lecturer, but he used a number of tools to get us to learn medieval rhetoric or whatever other course he taught. His standards were high and he had little tolerance for students unwilling to work.

Combining toughness with love, LaRusso really cared about each student. Italian to the core, he often referred to Dante's *Inferno* and cited the passage in which Dante reserves the lowest place in hell for people who ambled through life without developing their God-given talents. He wanted his students to stretch themselves as far as they could during his course.

Great teachers like LaRusso had a passion for their profession. Such passion left no doubt that they enjoyed, at a deep level, what they were doing. They respected and loved their students, held learning in high esteem and kept developing themselves as the years went on.

TEACHING AND SELF-DEVELOPMENT

The ancient philosopher Epicurus has received bad press over the centuries. Touted as the father of hedonism, Epicurus has been depicted as a pleasure-monger. But Epicurus was careful to distinguish between different kinds of pleasures. While he promoted moderate eating, drinking and sex, he also emphasized that pleasures of the mind yield greater satisfaction over a lifetime. He stressed that physical delights decline with the years, but those of the mind can go on well into old age.

More than most professions, education encourages its practitioners to nurture the mind. They know the joys of reading a good book or learning more about classical music.

Once cultivated, learning is one of the highest human pleasures. Teachers enjoy a double benefit because they learn and then transmit what they've learned to others. Highet puts it well when he says: "If you really understand an important and interesting subject, like the structure of the human body or the history of the two World Wars, it is a genuine happiness to explain them to others, to feel your mind grappling with their difficulties, to welcome every new book on them, and to learn as you teach."

The fulfilled teacher loves her profession because she continues to learn all through her life. Even the most educated person in the world knows only a fraction of what there is to know. My father practiced law for fifty-three years. He was fond of quoting the statement: "The beginning of wisdom is to realize how little we know." The most well-read scholar has read only a fraction of all the books housed in a public or university library. And the information in any library is a small portion of everything else that can be known. Learning something new every day is one of life's great and enduring pleasures.

Continuous learning is directly linked to one of the least satisfied human needs—self-actualization. Self-actualization is being all you can be and developing your talents. Self-actualization is the artist who paints as well as he can or the ballet dancer who keeps honing her talent. It's the writer who, after years of promising to write a book, finally does it and is proud of the effort. Self-actualization is the teacher who fulfills herself through constant learning and sharing what she knows with her students.

TEACHING PROVIDES BALANCE

Teachers come in all varieties—highly dedicated, lazy, committed and noncommitted. But the ones who seem most happy are the ones who know how to blend their profession into the other facets of their lives. Dedicated teachers get tired like anyone else who works fifty or more hours a week, but teaching is one of the best professions for fitting into the fabric of a well balanced life.

The Mayo Clinic in Rochester, Minnesota, has organized a program for burned-out professionals. Participants who are bone weary and brain numbed are asked to look at four quadrants in their lives—work, love, play, and worship. The four quadrants are placed in the form of a cross like the ones below in Figure 1.

Physician E. J. Kepler developed the cross. Kepler asks people to look at their own "cross" to see if it is balanced. If one professional is long on work and short on play, she can easily qualify as a victim of burnout and chronic fatigue. Someone else may have a lot of leisure because he has no job. The purpose of the exercise is to look at one's own life to see if it is balanced. If it is, the individual is usually much happier and less tired.

The "balanced cross" is similar to the principle, don't put all your eggs of happiness in one basket. Professionals who love their work often use it as a bulwark when other quadrants of their life start to crumble. A satisfying teaching career won't take away the pain of a shaky marriage, a painful divorce, or teenagers hooked on drugs; but contact with students

Figure 1: Balanced and Unbalanced Crosses

THE BALANCED CROSS

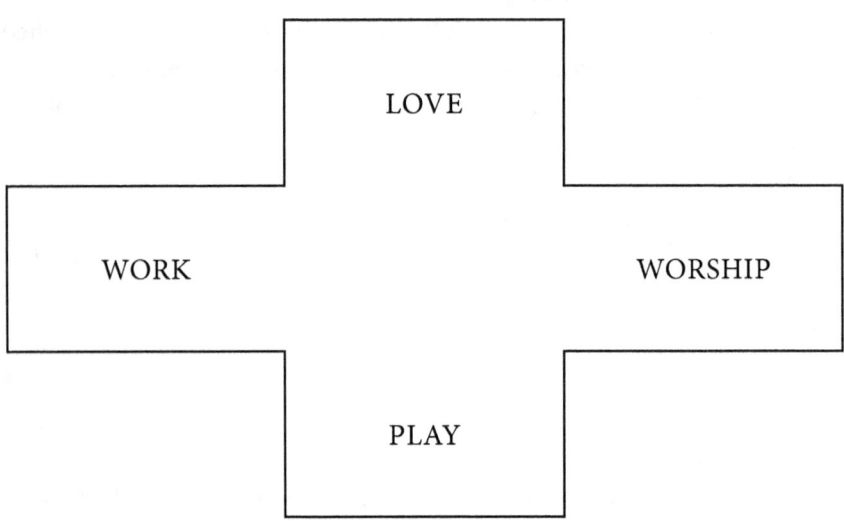

THE UNBALANCED CROSS

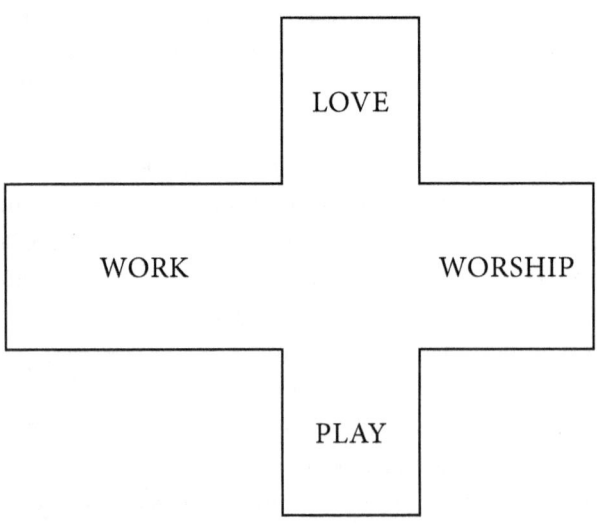

Why Is Teaching So Rewarding?

and colleagues, a sense of purpose, and immersion in a fulfilling job can help one get through the rough spots.

Thomas Edison said, "As a cure for worrying, work is better than whiskey." Freud maintained that to love and to work are twin essentials for a strong psyche. If one's work is simply a nine-to-five job endured only to bring home a paycheck, it's not very fulfilling. But if a teacher's profession produces deep fulfillment, she has discovered one of the secrets of a happy life.

2

Motivating Yourself to Teach

The hardest person you'll have to motivate is yourself.

THE RADIO ALARM GOES off at 5:45 a.m., and you don't appreciate the chipper voice of the deejay calling you to greet the day with a happy smile and the upbeat song he's about to play. You were up until midnight correcting papers because you had made an inane promise to students that you would return their essays by today. At that moment, somewhere between the body's scream for more sleep and your gnawing sense of duty, you grope for ways to psyche yourself up for another day of teaching. How do you do it?

One of a teacher's major jobs is to motivate students, but a far greater challenge is to persuade oneself. Even the best and happiest instructors have to fight burnout, tension, and apathy. But fight these demons they do and emerge better after the battle. What techniques do they use to motivate themselves every day not only to keep going back into the classroom but to like what they're doing year after year? The rest of this chapter will describe some of those techniques.

MOTIVATIONAL METHODS TEACHERS USE

I asked over one hundred American and Canadian teachers what they did to motivate themselves to keep going and to enjoy their profession. Answers were wide ranging and unique to each instructor. Sharleen Kapp teaches social studies to junior-high-school students in Calgary. Her primary source of motivation is the impact she has on students. She believes "teaching is a joy because I like what I do." She combines a strong love of learning with a dose of humor to keep both herself and her students motivated. She finds great satisfaction in improving the lives of her students: "Some of the kids I teach come from homes that have very little, and sometimes I feel badly for that. I took over my Calgary Flames hockey jersey and gave it to a fourteen-year-old boy's mother because I felt he needed it more than I. When I would see him in the halls wearing it, I knew I had done the right thing."

Kathleen Hazel finds that "with several family members in the field of education and having several inspiring teachers during my school days, I have never felt the need to be motivated to teach."

I was raised with a love of learning, and so my chief goal as an educator has been to instill that sensibility in my students. Broad-based knowledge first, goal-specific knowledge second. "A little knowledge is a dangerous thing . . . drink deep" (Alexander Pope).

Teaching has helped me to thrive intellectually and emotionally. Learning from others' wisdom and knowledge and differing perspectives has greatly augmented my life. That's a great motivator!

Case De Vries is a classroom teacher and department head in Quesnel, British Columbia. He applies computers to his courses and finds this keeps him and his students stimulated: "I've developed a real enthusiasm for computers, which I pass on to students, I use computers in developing newspaper units, teaching novels, and learning strategies."

Kathleen Ewing taught English composition classes at a community college and a private university. She admits, "the pay is lousy," but one way she keeps herself motivated is to "recall the power that certain teachers had on my life: and then I know that teaching does have importance. We can and do make a difference."

IS MONEY A MOTIVATOR?

Few teachers I interviewed said they chose their career for the money. Highet (*The Art of Teaching*) maintains that teachers worldwide live in "genteel poverty." Unlike opportunities in real estate, stocks, and precious metals, education offers no "get-rich" schemes. The teacher who has won the state lottery, inherited the family fortune, or who has a working spouse can live comfortably, but teaching is one of the lowest-paid professions for people with a four-year degree. While most teachers want and deserve a decent salary, money is not their key incentive. Finding meaning, touching lives, and self-development are their major reasons to teach.

SELF-MOTIVATIONAL METHODS

Teachers will spend far more time trying to persuade themselves than they'll ever put in motivating their students. We live with ourselves all the time and get no break from self. We may talk to students for many hours over an academic year, but that time is brief when compared with the time we spend conversing with ourselves. If we chart all the conversations we've had with other people and all the ones we've held with ourselves, it becomes obvious that we log many more hours with ourselves. People end other relationships all the time. They separate, get divorced, and leave in the summertime, but we can't do that with ourselves. We can't say to ourselves: "This relationship is not working out; let's get some space from each other for a while." If we don't have ways of motivating ourselves on a regular basis, we'll have a hard time staying fulfilled as teachers because too many obstacles go with the territory. Overwork, not enough hours, burnout, political hassles within the school, difficult students, and the challenge of going year after year can tax even the most dedicated educator.

Ray Raphael (*The Teacher's Voice*) discusses a trick teachers use to keep themselves motivated over a long career. It's called "The Quitting Game." Every year, certain educators tell themselves that this will be their last year. But when fall rolls around again, they're back in the classroom, energized by their students and the new year. Raphael maintains, "The more tricks, the better. In one way or another, teachers have to devise ways of coping with the passage of time in their professional careers." Raphael is right. Teachers need as many tactics as they can muster to stay fulfilled in the classroom.

THE POWER OF PERCEPTIONS IN STAYING MOTIVATED

One of my favorite cartoons appeared a while back in the *New Yorker*. It depicted two intellectual types sitting on the steps of an old Victorian house during a party. One said to the other: "My feeling is that while we should have the deepest respect for reality, we should not let it control our lives." There's a strong psychological principle in those words. We're far more influenced by our perceptions than we are by the real world. We see life through our own rose or mud-splattered glasses. Optimists view the world far differently than pessimists. If teachers habitually focus on the rewards of what they do, they're far more likely to stay in the profession.

Motivating Yourself to Teach

Near the back of the human mind is a device called the reticular-activating system. This mechanism filters the myriad pieces of information that compete for our attention. Without the reticular-activating system, we would suffer information overload. We concentrate on what we consider most important at any given moment. Most of the time, we can choose to dwell on what we want, although this takes discipline, since there are so many distractions invading our senses and competing for attention. To be motivated, we have to perceive the rewards of what we want. The stronger the perception, the better the chance of being motivated.

The same principles that work in motivating other people also apply to self. A good persuader can motivate others or self in at least four ways: (1) by helping to fulfill human needs (2) by focusing on the benefits of the message, (3) by overcoming objections, and (4) by getting a commitment to an action until it becomes a habit.

NEEDS

Psychologist Abraham Maslow lists human needs in a five-layered triangle, beginning with physiological needs, and going up to security, love, self-esteem, and self-actualization. Maslow places the needs in pyramid form for two reasons: first, the lower needs have to be satisfied before the higher ones can be met. If we feel really insecure, we're not going to be very open to a pitch that promises to help us self-actualize. Second, the lower needs are satisfied for most North Americans far more often than the higher ones. Physiological needs are met more often than needs of self-esteem. The three needs that apply most often for educators are love, self-esteem, and self-actualization. Teaching is a unique way to love, because the teacher is giving something worthwhile to others. Besides dispensing knowledge or helping a student learn a skill, the fulfilled educator helps develop a student's potential. The best teachers bring out the best in their students, and therein lies one major source of their joy. Teaching is a unique way to share insights and experience with others who will benefit from them.

Someone has said that happiness is like quicksilver: if we try to grab it, it squirts away. But if we try to serve others, happiness comes as a quiet by-product of that service. The old adage "tis better to give than receive" contains a basic truth. Giving love leads to self-esteem because we usually feel best about ourselves when we're giving rather than getting. Teaching offers the ideal environment to give. The same could be said about medicine and social work or a number of other professions, but education is one of the best ways to touch people's lives in a positive way.

Needs are the springboard of human motivation, but by themselves they won't motivate. A scientist might need food, but she may be so preoccupied with an experiment that she forgets to eat. Something has to occupy her attention in a compelling way before she becomes motivated. William James was one of the first to emphasize the importance of grabbing and keeping attention in order to persuade. Advertisers move consumers to desire a product by constantly dangling the product before them. Compel someone to think about a new car often enough and pretty soon he has to have it. The strongest persuasion moves from inattention, to attention, to preoccupation to obsession.

EMPHASIZING THE BENEFITS

If we want to persuade ourselves, we need to graft an image of the benefits we think we'll gain from an activity. Abstract principles don't work as well as vivid images. Such mental pictures have to highlight the benefits of what we want. If we subject ourselves to the pain of a flu shot, we'll do so because we imagine the benefits of avoiding the hacking cough, the fevered brow and the general malaise that makes two weeks of winter so miserable. What we focus on in our mind will determine how strongly we'll be motivated to do something. The more vividly we see the reward of any action, the stronger we'll want to do it. Take, for example, the act of speaking to a group of fellow faculty—one of the hardest challenges for many teachers. It's one thing to teach students every day: it's something quite different to give a ten-minute presentation to peers once a year. If we perceive the experience as one that provokes fear, anxiety, and possible humiliation, we won't be very motivated to get up and give the talk. But if we can focus on the rewards or benefits of making a presentation, the more likely we'll want to do it. Such rewards could include the satisfaction of a well-prepared talk given to fellow professionals whose opinion we value. Or it might be the knowledge that we took on something hard and did it well.

We move toward that which is riveted in our minds over a period of time. The more vivid the image, the more we're inclined to act. This pattern can work for both negative and positive experiences. If I fell off the garage roof when I was eleven, that image gets dredged up every time I go near any height over six feet. Phobias often have their root in some unpleasant childhood experience that keeps repeating itself in the mind. Since public speaking is still one of the greatest fears for most North Americans (well ahead of the fear of snakes, closed spaces, and heights), the average person will avoid speaking to a group if he sees it as a forum for failure. He concentrates on the day he forgot his lines back in the seventh grade, and that humiliating memory surfaces almost every time he thinks about standing up in front of an audience. If he focuses on the disadvantages, he won't have the spark to prepare his material. But if he can fix his mind on the rewards or benefits of giving a public presentation, he'll be spurred on to prepare his ideas. He focuses his thoughts on the rewards of meeting a challenge and overcoming it.

OVERCOMING OBJECTIONS

Sales experts talk about the close of the sale as the most difficult phase of selling. Customers who resist a salesperson's persuasion do so usually because of some objection hovering in their minds. The objection might be the price of a car. An objection is the thorn in the side of successful persuasion. Adept salespeople know this, and rather than avoiding objections, they try to draw them out so they can deal with them. A self-motivated teacher needs to do the same. If he dwells on the negative aspects of teaching, he won't be motivated to go into the classroom. The old adage about optimists and pessimists seeing the glass half full or half empty applies to objections. Any teacher could reel off a series of reasons for not teaching—the day-to-day hassles, students who don't care, subject matter made routine through years of repetition, lower salaries than other professionals with comparable education, etc. The way to overcome such objections is to identify them and then take some specific steps to turn them around. An instructor might say to herself "Sure, I'm tired, but I'll feel great after teaching my two afternoon classes because I'll give my students something they can use." Also, strongly motivated educators dwell far more often on the positive features of teaching than they do on the negative.

COMMITMENT

If we've ever signed up and paid money for an exercise class or a speed-reading course, we know the power of commitment in motivation. On our own, we won't take the class, but if we've handed over the money, we'll get involved. Scan the yellow pages of any phone book and notice the number of programs designed to motivate people to lose weight or get exercise. It doesn't take a genius to figure out that humans have to decrease calories and exert more energy to lose weight. But millions are convinced they have to spend money to do just that. Weight loss and physical fitness centers have become a national mania. The key to their success is getting disciples to make' a commitment. If we commit to something either by paying money or by telling others what we're doing, we're far more likely to follow-through.

A THREE-PART PLAN

Most people aren't motivated unless they follow a daily method. I want to suggest three that work: meditation, guided imagery, and positive self-talk coated with a sense of humor.

Abstract principles usually don't motivate as well as clear images grafted on the mind. Most humans need a proven technique that becomes a daily habit. One of the best is meditation. Meditation has been around for centuries and versions of it range from transcendental to monastic. Religious groups in both the eastern and western churches have used it as a way of finding God and inner peace. There are many ways to meditate, but the essentials are the same. Practitioners find a quiet place and clear their thoughts of everything except a single idea. Some take a passage from Scripture and focus on the meaning of the passage. Others pick out a mantra—a single word that allows them to control their thoughts. The most important feature of meditation is to dwell on one thought and try to eliminate all others. Meditation provides a solid framework for concentrating only on those thoughts the meditater chooses. If we can control our thoughts, we have much greater control over our actions because we usually act on what we think about. But it's hard to concentrate, because too many other thoughts compete for attention. A typical teacher jumps out of bed, fixes coffee, grabs the paper, lets the dog out, gets the kids up, fixes them cereal and bananas, takes a shower, starts the car, and weaves through traffic until she arrives at school. The teaching day is another round of mini-events, which requires nimbleness of mind and strong coping skills.

Benefits of Meditation

Most people resist trying meditation for two reasons: the time it takes and the impression that meditation is some kind of mystical exercise for gurus. But meditation is practical because it produces a number of benefits when practiced on a regular basis. Millions of professionals now meditate because they find themselves calmer and more productive in their work. They accomplish much more when they're refreshed and healthy. Try reading material for class preparation when you're drained and notice how long it takes and how much you retain. Look over that same material when you're refreshed and recall how easily it's absorbed. If you're a lark—or morning person—it's far better to go to bed when you're tired and then get up earlier the next morning. Night owls operate better in the late hours, but the principle is the same. Use your mind when your mind is rested: you grasp material faster and it sticks longer. Practiced for ten to fifteen minutes a day, meditation soothes the tired brain and brings solace to a body that has been pushing itself too far. The act of standing up in front of a class is physically and mentally tiring. Most teachers talk about how exhausted they are during the first week in September when school starts again. They also feel worn out just before Christmas and the end of the academic year.

Meditation provides a rest and vitality that is often better than the refreshment gained from sleep. It also enhances physical health. Physician Bernie Siegel (*Love, Medicine & Miracles*) refers to meditation and states: "I know of no other single activity that by itself can produce such a great improvement in the quality of life." He goes on to list other advantages such as relaxing; lowering or normalizing and increasing the ability to handle stress.

Guided Imagery

To stay motivated, people need a vivid image firmly fixed in their mind. The most eloquent teachers create colorful mental scenes of the Battle at Gettysburg or Hamlet's soliloquy for their classes. Students say they can "see" the battle or play in their minds. Teachers can use the same technique to motivate themselves.

Guided imagery works well right after meditation. An instructor can vividly imagine the teaching day and then focus on the rewards of what a teacher does. As clearly as possible, he maps in his mind everything that is going to happen from the moment he arrives at school until he leaves. The key element of the method is to see what is going to occur and then focus on the rewards. Athletes and dancers use this method to mentally rehearse upcoming events. Athletes see in their minds the game they're going to play. The basketball player envisions every phase of a successful free throw. The dancer visualizes each step she is going to take on stage.

Very few of us would accept a part in a play and then not learn our lines or try to get inside the thoughts and feelings of the character. Actors not only memorize their lines, but they burrow in their brains the thoughts and feelings of the characters they play. They put in hours trying to feel the emotions so they can project those emotions to their audience. This same process works for self-motivation. Psychologists who help people get over phobias have their clients vividly imagine the object of the fear and then mentally go through the steps of overcoming it. Someone has said, "Do the thing you fear the most and the death of fear is certain." An agoraphobic might imagine standing on the tenth story of a building and then looking down at the street below. Then he imagines himself in control of his fear and relishes the control he has of his emotions.

Abstract promises don't work very often. That's why most New Year's resolutions melt like snow in the sun by January 3. To find teaching a joy, I have to see myself in a specific scene. I then focus on the reward of a well-taught class and the benefits to students. If I begin each day by mentally going through what I am going to do and also dwell on the rewards of my actions, I'm going to be a lot more motivated. In the process, I find my job much more satisfying.

Positive Self-Talk Coated with a Sense of Humor

If the hardest person we have to convince is ourselves, then the language we use is crucial in staying motivated. Linguists emphasize that language shapes thought. If we call ourselves inept, aloof and incompetent, we'll probably act in ways that will confirm those words. If we tell ourselves that we're well-prepared, articulate and really love our students, those words should also propel us to act out what they mean. The internal conversations we carry on go a long way in shaping our self-image. A continuous stream of positive messages will almost always guarantee positive actions. A constant barrage of self put-downs will throw us into a deep blue funk.

Self-talk can take the form of affirmations like "I'm an excellent teacher because I know my subject," or "I can handle discipline problems in my classroom because I'm in control, and I've imagined the scene in advance."

GETTING THROUGH THE SLUMP TIMES

Even the best and most inspired educators have times when they spin into a slump—much like the great athletes who excel most of the time but who have a bad day, week or entire season.

The reasons for such a slump are many. For some, the same old schedule year after year wears down the most avid educator. For others, a change from a first-rate school to one which has major problems produces depression. For still others, a nagging illness makes it hard to stay enthused. Each teacher has her own reasons and set of circumstances. But certain methods seem to help rejuvenate a sagging spirit and tired body.

Victor Frankl (*Man's Search for Meaning*) offers one of the best approaches for overcoming the negative. He recounts his experiences as a psychiatrist who survived Nazi concentration camps by using the principle of "transcendence." Simply put, transcendence is a method of rising above difficult circumstances by fixing the mind on something more positive.

Frankl was a well-educated, sensitive man who was jerked from his comfortable world and thrown into the horror of Auschwitz. Unlike other physicians, he didn't get to treat the sick but was forced to do hard, manual labor. He tells how he and his fellow prisoners had to get up at 5 a.m., march for two hours in bitter cold, and then work for fourteen hours trying to dig out a highway in the frozen ground. He sustained himself by fixing his mind on something other than the conditions immediately confronting him. At times, he thought about his wife and her reassuring love, even though he wasn't sure she was alive. The vision of her strong affection and support kept him going. He states, "My mind clung to my wife's image, imagining it with uncanny acuteness. I heard her answering me, saw her smile, her frank and encouraging look. Real or not, her look was then more luminous than the sun which was beginning to rise."

Frankl also distracted himself from prison life by imagining that he was giving a lecture about his experiences once he was free. He recalls: "I forced my thoughts to turn to another subject. Suddenly, I saw myself standing on the platform of a well-lit, warm and pleasant lecture room. In front of me sat an attentive audience on comfortable upholstered seats. I was giving a lecture on the psychology of the concentration camp!" (ibid.)

Teachers don't have to endure a Nazi concentration camp, but they sometimes face demoralizing situations. Students pull knives, smart off in class, and shout in defiance. Personal lives get shattered through death, divorce, family turmoil, or hundreds of other trials humans face in this life. Meditation, guided imagery, positive self-talk and transcendence may not solve these problems, but they're proven tools in the battle to stay sane. Practiced together, they're powerful antidotes to weariness and depression.

PERSEVERANCE

Winston Churchill is well known as an inspirational speaker. Despite a constant personal battle against stage fright, Churchill delivered some of the finest talks in British history as he rallied his fellow countrymen to resist the Nazis. But he delivered one of his most famous—and shortest—orations to students at his alma mater in England. The students were waiting for the great man to talk at length. But Churchill arose, looked at the crowd, and proclaimed: "Never give up. Never give up. Never give up." Then he sat down.

Motivated teachers often live Churchill's succinct advice. Despite all the problems that go with education, they don't give up. Such perseverance provides a rich payoff in personal satisfaction and in the knowledge that students have learned something that will enrich their lives.

3

Motivating Students

"Apathy, apathy everywhere, but I don't care."
—Source unknown

THOMAS PRESSLY'S STUDENTS ALWAYS gave him an *A* in the annual course critique at the University of Washington. Students who missed his classes felt deprived. In his urbane, polished way, he motivated students to learn history. One student in Dr. Pressly's American History course described his teaching: "Pressly is a superb instructor—he is extremely well read; his lectures are well organized and easy to remember. He's the type of lecturer I would like to have in all lecture classes because he is so good." Another student in his Modern American Civilization course said: "Dr. Pressly is one of the few people in my life that I can say really inspired me" (Baird, ed., *Course Critique*).

How did Professor Pressly do it? What methods did he use to make learning something to be enjoyed rather than endured?

Students who walked into the lecture hall saw an outline of the day's lecture on the blackboard. As Pressly entered, he smiled at the group. He began his lecture by discussing the 1865 diary entry of a confederate soldier's wife. Pressly talked with feeling about the young woman's heartache and anxiety as she waited for her defeated husband to come home to their burned-out plantation in Georgia. Students paid attention as the teacher spoke. The story about the young Southern wife was the instructor's "grabber," and the 125 listeners sat transfixed as he delivered a well-organized lecture, filled with facts and historic trends, sprinkled with human-interest tidbits.

What makes the difference between a teacher like Thomas Pressly, who can hold students, and one who produces blank stares and suppressed yawns? All of us have known teachers who could make us sorry the class was over, and others who made us glad the bell rang. How do the effective ones motivate their charges to want to listen and learn? The rest of this chapter will focus on some obstacles to motivation and then include specific methods for motivating students.

I define *motivation* as a systematic attempt to keep students interested in material taught in class and to persuade them to like learning. An educator who can do both almost always has students who learn the subject matter.

Why is motivating students so hard? Eble (*The Craft of Teaching*) emphasizes that learning is a pleasant experience. Most educators agree with Eble, but they also know that many students haven't learned the good news yet (ibid). Legions of grade school and high-school students are in class because they have to be and can't wait for the day when they will "gain their freedom." Some might choose to be in school, but many would rather be almost anyplace else. Adults can recall their own longing in grade school for release in the summer. Anyone who confided on the playground that he liked school was ostracized or pegged as a nerd. You didn't brag to your buddies that you enjoyed school. You were pressured to claim that you hated being there and that your only source of solace was recess and after-school sports. Closet lovers of learning had to keep their condition to themselves.

MOTIVATING TEENAGERS

Influencing anyone is hard but adolescents are a special challenge. Teens struggle through the minefields of puberty, acceptance by peers, and a sense of who they are. They often resist advice from adults whose ideas seem outdated and repressive. Teenagers live out a paradox that makes it tough and easy to motivate them. They want their autonomy, but they still need emotional support from adults. Experts in adolescent psychology emphasize that teens are not so much trying to gain independence as a sense of identity. The "terrible twos" allowed them to start feeling independent. By the age of thirteen, most young people are asking, "Who am I?" "How do I fit in?" "Do my peers like and respect me?" By age nineteen, most students reclaim their benign dispositions. Parents and teachers rediscover some of the more appealing traits that distinguished the preadolescent. Adults who thought their teenagers had visited another planet are relieved to see the return to earth.

Good teachers try to understand the needs and developmental stages of their teenage students. Rather than seeing the bizarre clothing, outlandish hairstyle and bravado as signs of rebellion, they understand these manifestations as part of the rite of passage through a difficult phase. They study their charges carefully and choose the motivational methods they believe will work best.

THE CHALLENGE OF TELEVISION

Teachers have some stiff competitors for the minds of their students, but their biggest rival is television. Studies demonstrate that the average student will spend more time watching TV per year than she or he will spend in a classroom. The task of competing seems overwhelming. Most students choose to sit in front of the tube for hours—they almost never choose to come to school for classes. And once they get to the classroom, they find it hard to shut out the distractions they brought with them. Marshall McLuhan, the Canadian authority on the media, compares the television set to the ancient tribal fire where members of the village sat around mesmerized by the flames. Anyone who doubts the hypnotic power of TV should try interrupting devotees as they watch their favorite daytime drama. Interrupters are abruptly silenced, especially if they happen to enter the room just before Jason is about to tell Jessica he is going to leave her for Ramona before the baby is born.

Television has also changed the way students process information. Neurolinguistic programmers maintain that people filter data three ways: visually, auditorily and kinesthetically. Television has tipped the scales heavily toward the visual. If a child is brought up on a steady diet of *Sesame Street*, sitcoms, and sports, a kindergarten or first-grade teacher has an immediate challenge: how does she create the same level of interest and entertainment as the programs? How does she keep the action fast paced and continually moving? Compare the quick mosaic of messages and constant variety of information on *Sesame Street* to a typical first-grade classroom. Few teachers can keep up. Students raised in a family where the TV set is on ten hours a day find it hard to listen to sustained discourse. The pattern of constant images interrupted every few minutes by a commercial makes it hard for the most dedicated student to focus.

PROBLEMS IN LISTENING

Even if television weren't a strong competitor for a student's attention, keeping interest would still be a struggle. Listening is hard work. Nichols has shown that the average college student listens only about half the time during a typical lecture. Many students absorb only fifteen percent of what their teachers say. Even the best students listen to about 65% of a lecture. Students find it hard to pay attention all through a class. Many tune out a lecturer who has a monotonic or abrasive voice. They also daydream if an instructor presents abstract material with no specific examples to illustrate the principles. Most students have become adept at faking attention. They can look directly at the teacher with apparent fixation and wonder what soup the cafeteria is serving for lunch. Or they can be spinning out an intricate sexual fantasy at the moment they seem so concerned about the difference between a noun and a dangling participle.

So how do top teachers motivate students to listen and learn? Despite difficulties in listening and student resistance to teacher influence, some news is good. Students as a group are more open to persuasion than adults. Simons, has drawn a profile of the easiest and most difficult people to motivate. Those most vulnerable to influence have the following traits: they're young, have low self-esteem, are intolerant of ambiguity, and have relatively little education. Not all students fit that description, but many do. If teachers can get beyond the apathetic or cynical facade some students project, they'll find them receptive to instructors they like and respect.

LIKING AND MOTIVATION

The single strongest way teachers can motivate students is to like them. Robert Cialdini (*Influence*) devotes a chapter to what he calls "Liking, the Friendly Thief." Cialdini emphasizes that likeable people are more influential than their neutral or unlikeable counterparts. Liking students seems to be a given for teachers, but not all instructors really like their students. They teach because it's their job, or because it gives them the chance to develop their own needs. Also, there are degrees of liking. Most faculty members like most of their students, but a few really like every student they teach. They care deeply about each one and make the student their top priority. In return, most students respond in kind and because they like their teachers, will usually try to produce their best work.

Some teachers might protest that their primary job is not to be liked but to get students to learn. Such a claim has some validity: excellence in teaching has more to do with grasp of material and clear communication techniques than popularity. Likeability by itself does not guarantee excellent teaching. Most of us can remember an amiable instructor who courted students by telling war stories, letting classes out early and, in general, demanding little from the group.

The best teachers usually like their students and are also demanding. Such teachers have high standards as they push and prod their charges to give their best. Liking between teacher and students becomes a powerful motivator on both sides of the desk. The relationship between the student and teacher is similar to any other strong relationship. We're attracted to and motivated by people who like us.

Fear and anxiety can be short-term motivators, and some teachers use these tactics to get students to learn. But in the long run, the teacher who combines high standards with genuine concern for students will have the most staying power. Such educators will also enjoy teaching far more than colleagues who tolerate or dislike students.

ADAPTING MOTIVATIONAL METHOD TO INDIVIDUALS

If liking students is the strongest motivator, the next is adapting persuasive methods to individual students. Thousands of attempts to motivate fizzle because instructors don't try to get inside the heads and hearts of those they want to influence. One of the biggest mistakes people make is to assume that others hold their world-view. If pinned down, they would say "No, of course I believe others think and learn differently than I do." But this principle is often forgotten when motivating students. Effective motivators carefully analyze the attitudes of their listeners and then adapt their approach to what they find. Educators who motivate their students to pay attention and to enjoy learning use the same approach. They begin by deciding on learning objectives during a given semester, week or class period. Then, they spend time choosing those appeals that work best with their group of students. Master teachers know that students have different styles of learning. Some learn through practical experience, others by watching and reflecting, still others through abstract thinking, and some by actively experimenting. Give five fourteen year olds the task of learning how to use an Apple computer and watch the way they try to master the machine. A few will ignore the instruction manual and start tinkering with the keys. Three or four more wouldn't think about touching the computer until they had thoroughly read the instructions. A few use a combination of reading and experimenting

The good teacher takes time to find out how students in a class learn best, and then she adapts. She knows she can't always tailor her strategy to every student, especially when she has a large class, but her awareness of different learning styles allows her to hit the mark more often than an instructor who acts as though all students process information the same way.

The best teachers stay on the lookout for materials—stories, news items, fashions, trends—they know their students find intriguing. They combine the right mix of preparation, examples and communication skills to make the material both clear and compelling.

An English teacher wants her senior-high-school students to focus on revenge in Shakespeare's *Hamlet*. So she looks for an approach that will appeal to this group. She may know that these seniors are struggling with the emotion of revenge because some of their members had been physically attacked by students from another school. She then focuses on that incident and uses it as a catalyst for discussing Hamlet's feelings of revenge toward his father's murderer. She may go on to emphasize that Hamlet's anger against King Claudius—the suspected murderer—was so intense that he hesitated to kill the king while Claudius was at prayer: Hamlet feared that death at prayer might send Claudius to heaven when he wanted him to go to hell. The instructor might then involve the class in a discussion of what revenge does to the person planning it. She might ask her class what the feeling of revenge does to them. Does it produce something good, or does it fill them with anger? How was Hamlet affected by his all-consuming desire to murder Claudius? Did the prince of Denmark destroy himself in the process of killing someone else?

ATTENTION DETERMINES ACTION

After analyzing the attitudes of students, effective motivators grab their attention. Humans are bombarded by thousands of messages each day, but only a few command attention. A speaker who gets an audience to focus on a single idea has taken a major step in motivating students. Professor Pressly was a master at getting 125 students to fix their eyes and minds on him and the material he was teaching. He captured their attention at the beginning and kept it with human-interest examples, superb organization, and practical applications.

MOTIVATE BY BUILDING: SELF-ESTEEM

Steve was a fourth grader, and despite constant attempts made to help him, he still couldn't read or write. Dr. Curtis Leadbetter started working with Steve. Curt is an optimist who teaches at Brigham Young University. He used a simple motivational technique. He asked the student to begin each day by saying to himself "God loves me. I'm a winner. I can read and write." He also gave him a penny to put in his shoe and told him "Every time you feel the penny, repeat the same words 'God loves me. I'm a winner. I can read and write.'" Within two months, Steve had made remarkable progress. Fellow educators found it hard to believe that such a simple method could produce a turnaround, but it did.

Appeal to self-esteem is one of the strongest human needs. Advertisers know this principle well and use it to sell products. It's illogical to believe that a toothpaste will make someone more appealing to members of the opposite sex, but this ploy has worked for decades. Strong teachers don't flatter to bolster a sagging self-esteem, but they look for opportunities to make students feel good about themselves and their accomplishments. Top teachers praise when students do something well. They usually focus on the work and not the student who did it. Instead of saying "You're a good writer," they say, "This essay is well written because it's concise and full of descriptive detail."

Sister Phyllis Taufen taught junior-high students for years. She has been an assistant professor of English at Gonzaga University. In 1988 she won the Burlington Northern award for teaching excellence. I asked her to describe her approach to teaching. She responded "Excellence is my goal and affirmation is my means." She sets high standards for college students who take her business-writing class, but she emphasizes that "every day a student should go home feeling successful." Sister Phyllis affirms the strong features of each paper and then gives specific directions for strengthening the weak points. She emphasizes the link between competence and confidence. If a student thinks he writes well but doesn't, he's in for a rude jolt when he turns in a sloppy essay or tries to fill out a job application. But if he knows how to write well because he has worked hard and improved, his confidence is built on solid ground.

MOTIVATE BY BEING ENTHUSIASTIC

Father Gerald Steckler was a pied piper with a passion for his subject. He held strong views that the world was getting worse each day. In his somber but witty way, he emphasized that global disaster was imminent. The only thing he didn't do to promote his doomsday philosophy was to carry a sign that read, "The end is near." So what explains his immense popularity with students? They flocked to his courses and sat mesmerized as he spun his tales of foreboding. Fr. Steckler's secret was an enthusiasm for his subject and his ideas. Such enthusiasm was relayed to his classes. His course crackled with excitement and his students listened, learned and, in many cases, accepted his viewpoint.

Teachers can project enthusiasm in different ways. For some, the energetic voice relays the message that the subject matter is important. For others, body language and facial expression transmit the message that they believe in what they're doing. Very few of the great teachers come across as neutral in a classroom. Such enthusiasm is infectious and motivates students to pay attention and absorb.

BE CREATIVE AND USE A VARIETY OF TEACHING METHODS

Successful teachers are always finding new ways to put their material across. They know that variety is the spice of instruction. During a class period they might lecture, use hands-on involvement, a visual aid, and a class project. Throughout the term, they keep students intrigued because they change their method to fit the group and subject matter.

Variety is crucial during a class session that lasts longer than an hour. A few years ago, I was asked to teach a graduate course. A group of Air Force officers wanted Gonzaga University to offer master's-level classes, but they wanted them taught on weekends. Most of the students were pilots and navigators stationed at Fairchild Air Force Base near Spokane. Two intensive weekends fit the officers' schedule best since they had to stay on military alert at the base. The first weekend was set up to meet from 6 to 10 p.m. on Friday night, 9 to 5 on Saturday, and 9 to 5 on Sunday. After an intervening weekend, students and instructor repeated the same format.

Motivating Students

The two intensive weekends covered the required number of hours, but it was a challenge to keep instructor and students motivated for such long blocks. Planning, variety, and involvement became our survival tools. I learned more about how to teach during those marathon sessions than during any other time. The class was called Group Theory, and it focused on group problem-solving methods. On Friday night from 6 to 8, I gave lectures, with room for plenty of feedback from students. By 8 o'clock, when most normal humans were going to football games or finding some other way to unwind after a workweek, all of us were numb. So I showed a twenty-eight-minute movie about the Nazi invasion of France in 1938. The movie demonstrated the Allies' failure to thwart the attack. I then asked the students, who now had the advantage of hindsight, to decide how to stop the Nazis. Three separate groups held a discussion for a half hour. Then each group presented its solutions and compared its approach with the other two groups. We tried to put the best thinking of all three together into one unified solution.

Most of the time, this exercise worked because the participants got involved, despite their weariness. Even the nonmilitary students who attended were energized by the challenge of stopping the Luftwaffe. Four straight hours of lecture would have produced an incoherent instructor talking to a comatose audience.

I used a varied approach on Saturday and Sunday. In the morning, I gave a lecture-discussion followed by a problem-solving group exercise. In the afternoon, I lectured for forty-five minutes and then showed a movie on leadership. (Movies right after lunch are dangerous because the dark room allows viewers to sleep without detection.) The film was followed by a discussion and then another group exercise.

Most teachers don't limit themselves to a single teaching style. They use a lecture if it works well with one group of students. But if they notice that a series of lectures produces yawns, slumped bodies, and listless stares, they change strategy. If they have to teach a course that lasts more than an hour, they look for ways to keep the class moving.

MOTIVATE BY TELLING STORIES

One of the oldest and most creative ways to gain and keep students' attention is through the use of stories. Jewish storyteller Steve Sanfield (*Could This Be Paradise?*) tells about Jacob Ben Wolf Kranz who was born in 1741 in the small town of Zietil in the Vilna district of Lithuania. Before he was twenty-one, he was regarded as an accomplished scholar. But he was also known as a great orator and teacher. He exhorted his fellow Jews to greater devotion with parables and stories. One day his good friend, Rabbi Elijah of Vilna, asked him how he managed to find the right parable for every subject and every situation. Rather than reply with a lengthy explanation, the Preacher of Dubno told the following story.

There was once a Russian nobleman who was obsessed with the art of archery. It was his goal to become the master archer of his time. He attended all the military academies, studied with the great teachers, even journeyed to the far corners of the empire to consult with the masters of the long bow. This went on for years. And although he became more skillful than most, he never achieved his dream of hitting the bull's eye every single time. Once, he was traveling past a small Jewish town. There on the side of an old barn were two dozen crudely painted targets. And in the middle of each and every bull's eye was an arrow. The nobleman was amazed. Never had he seen such a display of marksmanship. Immediately, he had the one responsible brought before him, and he was even more amazed when the archer turned out to be a young barefoot boy dressed in rags. "You, you did this?" the nobleman asked in astonishment. "Yes your Excellency," the boy said softly. "Remarkable, remarkable! Where did you develop such skill? How did you do it?" "It's simple, your Excellency. First I take careful aim, I let the arrow fly and after it hits the barn, then I paint the target around it." "And so," concluded the Preacher of Dubno, "I proceed much in the same manner as the boy did. Whenever I come upon a good parable or an interesting story, I hold it in my mind until eventually I find the right situation to paint around it." Another time, a group of townspeople came to the preacher and said, "We admire your learning and your scholarship. We also admire your parables. But we question if they are really necessary. After all, Judaism is based on plain and simple truths. Why should these truths be hidden in parables, which often confuse the facts?" The preacher answered with another parable. Truth used to walk around naked. People were shocked and outraged. They turned their backs on Truth and refused to listen to him. Wherever he went, he was either rejected or ignored. One day, when he was sadly walking down a back street, trying to keep out of everyone's way, he met Parable, all decked out in bright clothes. Truth poured out his bitter heart, "It's not fair! Why do you get so much attention when everyone ignores me?" "Well friend," replied Parable, "the problem is: you walk around plain and unadorned. People just don't like to meet you naked, face-to-face. If you let me help you, you'll see a big change in your life." Parable then gave Truth some of his beautiful clothes. Suddenly, Truth was elegant and attractive. After Truth joined hands with Parable, he was welcomed by everyone who saw him.

"And that," said the Preacher of Dubno, "is what I try to do for Truth in my parables. I do not change the truth, nor, heaven forbid, confuse it. I simply dress it in beautiful clothes. With or without my parable, truth remains the same. But by making it more appealing, truth is able to enter the hearts of everyone."

If you find a good story, save it until you can match it to a point you want to make. Stories flavor abstract ideas and make them far more appealing. By themselves, principles are often dull. With the stories, they come alive. Because stories grab and hold attention, weaving anecdotes into classes often works better than merely explaining principles. Students can grasp images in a parable but they often have to grope to understand ideas without the help of an illustration or a story. Abstract principles are like Teflon: they don't stick. Stories or parables are like Velcro: they have holding power long after the class is over.

Writing experts urge beginning writers to "show and not tell." To show means to paint graphic pictures like the two preceding stories about the archer and Truth. Successful writers show because they have a much better chance of getting their readers to stay with them throughout the article or book. Readers are generally an impatient lot. Bore them in the opening paragraph and they'll stop reading. Launch into an abstract discussion in the middle of the essay, and they'll think about something else. Stories by themselves don't guarantee learning. Most of us can recall teachers who spun personal anecdotes that had nothing to do with the subject matter. We may have enjoyed the diversion as the teacher told us about the time he scored the winning touchdown for Sabre Jet High School, but we didn't learn much. Effective teachers motivate to pay attention by blending concepts with examples. Imagination fuels the mind. Abstract principles slip away unless they're anchored by graphic illustrations. Recall our best teachers and we'll most likely remember first-rate storytellers.

MOTIVATE BY PROMOTING THE BENEFITS OF LEARNING

Top salespeople don't try to sell products as much as they promote the benefits of the product. A good insurance agent will focus on the motorist's peace of mind that comes with automobile coverage. She doesn't concentrate on the facts and figures of the policy but demonstrates how her company will provide the best protection and the least worry. Good teachers use the same approach as they promote the benefits of material learned in class. Some educators are reluctant to "sell" their material because they believe their job is to dispense knowledge. A few will argue, with some merit, that knowledge doesn't have to be practical, but should be learned for its own sake. But students, like anyone else, will be more motivated to listen and learn if they know why they're studying algebra or economics or sociology. If they see a payoff, they'll be far more likely to tune in to what is going on in class. Effective teachers are not reluctant to reinforce how important it is to master their subject matter. Besides explaining mathematical equations, an instructor might underscore the importance of math and science in today's world. A history teacher might reinforce Santayana's dictum that "whoever ignores history is bound to repeat its mistakes." Writing teachers often emphasize the necessity of clear, concise writing in business. Logic teachers show the close link between decision-making and a grasp of syllogisms, fallacies and arguments. Students are like consumers who purchase products. They're much more ready to buy if they see a good reason for doing so.

MOTIVATE BY ADAPTING AS MUCH AS POSSIBLE TO EACH STUDENT'S NEEDS

In persuasion, no one approach fits all. The speaker who tries to convince a large audience to accept his position on abortion may strike a chord with some members, but he will just as surely alienate others—unless everyone already agrees with what he's promoting. Like anyone else, students are unique and respond to different approaches.

It's often impractical, if not impossible, to adapt to each student's needs, but the more a teacher can do so, the better chance she has of motivating. Robert Conklin advises, "To the degree you give others what they want, they will give you what you want" (*How to Get People to Do Things*).

MOTIVATE WITH CONSTRUCTIVE CRITICISM

Good teachers know how to mix praise and criticism in the right dosage. An instructor who always builds up and never critiques might make students feel better about themselves, but is neglecting a strong motivational method. Criticism tempered with love and applied at the right time often works to spur students to improve. Former Notre Dame football coach, Lou Holtz, is a master motivator because he knows how to use negative feedback and when to avoid it. Each comment is designed for a specific purpose. If the coach believes that one player will respond better with praise, that's what he gets. If someone else will improve with constructive criticism, he'll hear negative feedback. Coach Holtz gives his quarterbacks a hard time in practice because he knows if they can take his harassment, the game should be easy.

Much of our educational system is built on the foundation of constructive criticism. A drama director shapes and chisels her young actors until they polish their performance. A writing teacher keeps handing back an essay until it's clear, concise, and well developed. A biology teacher won't accept a lab report until it's done right. Some students are surprised and disappointed if they don't get feedback because they don't believe they're learning.

Like praise, effective criticism is a strong motivator if it is directed at the activity and not the person. The teacher who merely demeans often has a shattered student ego to reassemble. A drama coach shouts "You are the slowest actor I have ever had to work with! Will you ever get that line right?!" The student actor may react by feeling devastated, but he's so consumed with the feeling of humiliation that he doesn't focus on how to get the part right. The effective coach concentrates on the behavior that needs changing and mixes his comments with something positive. A good writing teacher doesn't say, "You're a very vague writer" but suggests instead, "Could you make these two sentences clearer? I had a hard time understanding them."

Praise or criticism work best when they're coated with a generous supply of love. If a relationship is bonded by strong affection, participants can handle conflict, disagreement, or an occasional fight. But if the bond is fragile or nonexistent, people find it hard to accept any conflict or negative criticism. Children can tolerate discipline easily if they feel loved. If they're not loved, they flinch at the slightest put-down.

One guideline for criticizing is to communicate the feedback individually to the student who needs it. Often this approach isn't practical because it's too time consuming for a coach to talk to each player or for a drama instructor to wait until after rehearsal to give a critique. But if it is practical, individual criticism has the advantage of getting the student to focus on the behavior or material that needs work and not on the embarrassment of getting skewered in front of fellow students.

You might recall a speech class in which the instructor would wait until the inexperienced and nervous speaker finished his talk and then said: "That was a good speech except for the following faults which I would now like to highlight." After a five minute critique, the instructor then turned to the rest of the class and said, "Now how else can we help this person get over his flaws?" The student may have heard some of the criticism, but he was also busy trying to cope with his sense of inadequacy rather than trying to apply the negative feedback from teacher and classmates. Privately written comments on a speech outline or an essay often help beginners concentrate on what needs to be changed. Then, periodically, an instructor can discuss with the whole class common problems that apply to a set of speeches or papers.

Another effective approach is to ask students to critique themselves. A student speaker, for example, can learn more in five minutes of watching a videotape of herself than she can in listening to ten minutes of feedback from an instructor. Self-criticism joined with instructor feedback also works. The student provides a self-critique and then the teacher either confirms or denies what the student says. A student's self-critique is often more harsh than an instructor's. Then, the instructor can assume the role of confidence builder by pointing out the virtues of the talk.

Effective teachers use whatever method they believe will best develop an individual student. One student might respond better to a constant stream of positive comments about a project. Another reacts best with a combination of praise and constructive criticism. A third improves with self-criticism and teacher feedback.

Motivation works when a teacher tailors the right strategy to the individual needs of students. Like the pro golfer who uses the iron or putter that will get the ball in the cup, a successful teacher carefully considers what motivational approach she should use and then applies it. The best teachers also tune into the learning styles of students and adapt accordingly. They vary their approach to keep students interested.

Motivating Students

Proven techniques won't work with every student and every class. Experienced instructors have learned that like any other relationship in their life, the one between teacher and students can range from euphoric to disastrous. No one class or one student is exactly alike. In some courses, a teacher can establish rapport from the first minute and the honeymoon continues until the last day. Such experiences linger long and happily in the minds of teachers and help account for the deep satisfaction of a career in education. But even outstanding teachers can recall classes and individual students who were more of a trial than a joy. Whether it was a lack of personal chemistry or in-built resistance by the students, the teacher couldn't form a bond. She might have done everything she normally does with classes that clicked, but this one was different. What was normally a positive experience turned out to be a negative one.

So what to do? Don't worry about it. The best teachers in the world don't appeal to every student they teach. They're the best because they consistently use proven principles of motivation and the law of averages works in their favor. Most students respond well to good teachers, but not all do. The key to survival in these rare instances is to keep a sense of humor and to repeat the phrase "This too shall pass." Teaching has the advantage of giving an educator a chance to start anew every term or academic year. Unlike someone who is stuck in an intolerable job with the same cranky co-worker for years, the teacher can learn from each difficult experience and get better with the next class.

4

Tools to Teach

The Lecture, Discussion, Dialectic, Textbook, and Computer

> "Students will tire of anything, even humor or anecdotes, if it is done for too long without a change of pace."
>
> —Joseph Lowman

THE TOPIC WAS WELL publicized and students gathered to hear one of the most famous speakers of the day. But by the time he had finished, only one of the listeners was still there—the rest had walked out. The lecturer was Plato, and the one student who stayed until the end was Aristotle. As far as we know, this was the first and last lecture Plato delivered. Aristotle later explained the unenthusiastic response. The topic was announced in advance as a discussion of "the Good." The Athenian students thought the speaker was going to discuss some practical ways to find pleasure, but instead Plato spoke about the transcendental soul. (Smith, et al., *Lives in Education*, 75–76) Most teachers haven't endured the experience of watching the audience get up and leave, but they know the feeling of addressing apathetic listeners. In the last chapter, I discussed ways of motivating students. In this chapter, I want to examine some tools a teacher can use to both motivate and instruct.

THE LECTURE

We don't know exactly what Plato said or how he delivered his ideas, but he took a chance when he lectured. Educators over the centuries have probably used the lecture more than any other tool. The format is still popular, especially at large universities. But the lecture is a two-edged sword. Goldhaber says: "Despite its known ineffectiveness as a teaching technique and as a linear communication activity, universities still use the lecture as the primary means of educating students. With the increasing emphasis on higher enrollments, budget cuts, and loss of faculty positions, the lecture is attaining new prominence as the most economical way to teach large numbers of students. Other potential drawbacks of the lecture include one-way communication to a group of passive listeners, few attempts to see if students are learning the material, and no hands-on application (Goldhaber, *Organizational Communication,* 460). But if used well, the lecture can be an excellent teaching tool. Lowman states that the "lecture also survives because at its best it can be magnificent." Properly delivered, a lecture lights up a room. If a teacher is well organized, presents her ideas clearly and sprinkles theory with riveting examples, she has a good chance of keeping the attention of her students. But if she speaks in a monotone, wanders all over her subject and hovers in the clouds of abstraction, most of her students will tune out. The bland lecture competes with the Quaalude as a way to induce sleep.

So what makes an effective lecture? In the words of McKeachie, a good lecture should be more than "a dreary set of facts . . . or a rehash of the textbook" (*Teaching Tips*, 24). A good lecture is usually a blend of principles, illustrations, graphics, and student involvement delivered in a vigorous style. McKeachie recommends that an instructor start by presenting a problem that needs a solution. Then he provides information that will help students find the answer themselves. The problem-solution approach involves the class far better than a recital of facts, formulas, or historical dates. Specific facts are like leaves on a tree—they have to hang on a branch to live. They also get their life from the tree. Facts in a lecture come alive when they're attached to a format like problem solving.

Students will remember specific information longer if a teacher gets them involved. A history instructor wants to present the fourteenth century dispute between the Dominican monk, Savonarola, and Pope Alexander VI. If he asks his class to memorize twenty-five facts about the conflict, students will be hard- pressed to remember the material later. But if the teacher presents the facts and dates as part of a problem that students need to solve, the specific data is much easier to understand and recall later. Ask class members to reel off the names and dates of an historic event, and they draw a blank. But intertwine the facts with a problem and students listen, get mentally involved and learn. Franklin underscores the drawing power of the problem format in attracting and keeping readers. He recommends a three step process: complication, development and resolution.

If an instructor wanted to use Franklin's method in the Savonarola/Alexander conflict, he might start by explaining the conflict: Savonarola was disgusted with what he saw as the absolute corruption in Florence and Rome. In his fiery sermons, he not only denounced worldly pleasures but excoriated the pope who seemed to enjoy them so much. The target of his diatribes was Pope Alexander VI, the man many historians tag as the most scandalous of pontiffs.

After some diplomatic attempts to tell Savonarola to keep his views to himself, the pope ordered the feisty monk to stop preaching. The ruling family of Florence, the Medici, backed Alexander because their city was the cradle of the Renaissance. Italians in the fifteenth century were starting to enjoy the fruits of art and literature passed on by the Greeks and Romans. Revelry and enjoyment of the finer things were becoming a way of life in Rome and Florence. Savonarola ignored the papal orders and continued to preach against earthly pleasures and to prophesy that doom would strike the Italians if they didn't change their ways. He also kept up his attacks on the leader of the church because he thought the pope was a bad example for the flock of Peter. Thus, the battle lines were drawn with the gaunt ascetic squaring off against the powerful and worldly pope.

The teacher presents the historical data as part of a conflict that needs a resolution. The approach gets students involved from the beginning and encourages them to think. The instructor adds probing questions to get class members even more involved. He asks: who was right? why didn't Savonarola give in to the pope and avoid all the turmoil? where do you think the clash will lead? A problem approach with questions leads students down the path of inquiry and makes them want to find out how the conflict ended. Stimulated by curiosity, they want to know the outcome if they've been participants in the process. After discussing the questions, students learn that Savonarola was tortured and executed. They can then discuss the key issues that emerge from the conflict: Was Savonarola right? Was his timing off? (Twenty years later Martin Luther would make some of the same charges.) Was Savonarola morally right but strategically wrong? How could he have achieved his goal of reform and not get killed in the bargain?

A successful lecture-discussion is like a good speech. It starts with a grabber, then offers a thesis, which the teacher develops in clear detail, and it ends with a definite conclusion. It contains all the necessary historic facts needed to understand the main issues. A good lecture can be wrapped in a number of formats like the problem-resolution or topical format, but it usually resembles a well-organized speech, which mixes principles with intriguing facts and some give-and-take between instructor and students.

A human-interest story or two embellishes almost any lecture. In the case of Savonarola and Alexander, a teacher might talk about Savonarola's power as a preacher. Despite his reedy voice and frail figure, the Dominican monk was able to rivet the attention of the listeners who sat in the Duomo, the main cathedral in Florence. He was particularly graphic in predicting some of the catastrophes that would strike Italy if listeners didn't heed his words. Some members of his audiences were so engrossed that they sighed and fainted at the sight of the fragile ascetic. After one of his scathing sermons, bands of idealistic teenagers bolted from the cathedral and scoured Florence for anything they considered worldly. Then they burned objects they considered sinful—paintings, clothing, and books that would have become fine works of art had they survived.

A teacher's delivery during a lecture doesn't have to be dramatic, but it helps. The voice should convey a sense of excitement and importance about the subject. She speaks slowly enough to be clearly understood but her rate isn't plodding. If she has the flair of an actress, she may imitate one of the historical characters she discusses in a lecture.

Master teachers are like outstanding theater performers. They raise and lower their voices, project emotion, and make their body movements match their delivery. Lowman (*Mastering the Techniques of Teaching*) emphasizes that the best college teachers use their classrooms much like a stage: "College classrooms are fundamentally dramatic arenas in which the teacher is the focal point, just as the actor or orator is on a stage. The students are subject to the same influences—both satisfactions and distractions—as any audience."

Many teachers are not dramatic in their approach and are still very effective pedagogues. But students often remember their best instructors as colorful performers who could grab a class's attention and hold it to the end of the session.

TO AVOID LOSING STUDENTS, CLIMB DOWN THE ABSTRACTION LADDER

Students often tune out because the teacher presents material in such an abstract way. The class struggles to understand key points. At the end of the fifty minutes, many of them have a jumble of notes but they don't know what the notes mean. The instructor has spoken about "social relevance," "prime matter and substantial form" and "totalitarianism" and students have nodded in feigned understanding. But except for the brightest and most dedicated, few have understood what the terms mean.

One way to avoid the problem of vagueness is to come down the abstraction ladder. Hayakawa explains this useful teaching device. Some words and ideas are specific and concrete: others are abstract. For example, "Napoleon Bonaparte" is specific because there has been only one Napoleon Bonaparte, famous French military leader.

The term "military leader" is more abstract because it includes many more people than Bonaparte. "Leader" includes as many leaders as there are or have been in the world. "Historic figure" is more abstract still. "Person" is another rung up on the ladder. "Thing" is the most abstract word because the term can include anything.

Below are the concepts in ladder form:

Thing

Person

Historical figure

Leader

Military leader

Napoleon Bonaparte

Abstractions can save time in communicating and are fine if everyone knows what the abstraction means. For example, a teacher doesn't have to name every student in the room if he wants to refer to the whole group. He can say "class," and no one misunderstands him. But if he's talking about "this class of objects," and he doesn't define the words *class* or *objects*, then students are lost.

Abstractions are also useful if students have been through the material and already understand difficult concepts. A political science teacher who has explained Marx's concept of "dialectical materialism" can use the term because the class knows what it means. But in presenting new abstract material, it helps to come down the ladder.

Say a teacher is explaining a concept like Aristotle's principle of "matter and form." He starts with a definition of the terms, but then quickly moves down the ladder with an analogy. For example, Aristotle maintains that every material object has some spiritual principle that informs it. Pretty abstract, no? But if the instructor descends the ladder and demonstrates that a car is both a sum of its material parts (matter) and also contains the ideas of its designer (form), the principle might become a little clearer.

Going down further, the teacher shows that the designer first had the idea of a particular car in mind—a Toyota Celica. Somewhere in Japan, the designer thought about the form the car should take and then transferred the idea to a blueprint. Celicas rolling off the assembly line are products of the designer's original idea. Thus "matter" is the sum of all the material parts; "form" is the thinking that went into making them fit together into a car that runs well. If a first-grader asks what "courage" means, the teacher wouldn't say "courage means fortitude." She might say that courage means "not being afraid of the dark when someone turns out the lights."

Stories and parables are good ways to climb down the abstraction ladder. One of the major reasons for Christ's success as a teacher was his use of parables. Unlike the scribes and Pharisees who often presented religious truths in abstract jargon, Christ talked about fig trees, lost coins and innkeepers. His listeners didn't have to struggle to grasp what he was saying. He didn't use terms like "eschatological" and "heuristic." He took complicated ideas and explained them in clear, simple statements.

Joseph Lowman spent two years watching and interviewing twenty-five college professors who were known as outstanding teachers. While the professors had their own individual styles, they shared some common approaches. One was their ability to present abstract material in a simple way. Lowman goes on to note: "Similarly, the ancient Greek and Hebrew teachers were masters of metaphor, making complex points by using simple language and concrete images.

EYE CONTACT DURING A LECTURE

A good preacher rivets his eyes on one person during a sermon—but only for a few seconds. An effective lecturer often does the same. Rather than letting her eyes sweep the audience like a spectator watching a tennis match, she looks at one student and then another. She carries on an animated conversation with individual members of her class. There are two good reasons for maintaining eye contact during a lecture: (1) students are more likely to pay attention to someone who establishes a visual bond, and (2) the instructor usually finds it easier to talk to one person than a sea of faces.

One device professional speakers use to channel nervousness and create a bond with their listeners is to find the friendliest face in the crowd and then talk to that person for a few seconds. Then she moves on to someone else who is smiling and nodding. She doesn't ignore the others, but she doesn't start with an audience member who looks apathetic or hostile. If she begins by looking at the bored and cynical members in the crowd, she can find her own confidence dropping. Most people are fluent when they speak to someone who gives them positive feedback. They get tongue-tied during a conversation with someone who intimidates them. They're too worried about the impression they're making rather than what they're saying.

One of the fastest ways for a teacher to bore himself and the class is to repeat, in a monotone, the same lecture term after term. The caricature is well established of the college professor standing behind the podium and reading from frayed, yellow lecture notes. Occasionally, he looks up from the ancient pages and makes eye contact with a student or two, but most of the time, he's buried in his scrolls.

The Need for Class Preparation

The best instructors prepare classes carefully, even if they've presented the same material before. They look for new and fresh ways to put the concepts across. They analyze the particular class they teach and adapt to them because they know that each group is different. A class of happy extroverts will quickly get involved, while a more quiet group will need prodding. Most seasoned teachers use an outline rather than a manuscript. Manuscripts take a long time, are tedious and lock an instructor into a word for word recitation. Besides, an instructor who burrows into a manuscript can't establish and maintain eye contact with students.

An outline of the class session allows the teacher to be flexible. An instructor can go off on a tangent. But she can always return to the outline if the ideas start to meander. The outline also invites fresh new material to illustrate ideas. If a teacher is trying to communicate the importance of textiles in thirteenth-century France, the outline can contain the major facts about trade and manufacturing. But each semester, he can add fresh new examples to liven up what he considers to be dull dry material. For example, an economics teacher might compare textiles in thirteenth-century France to microcomputer chips in the Silicon Valley. He constantly scans newspapers for material that might fit what he's trying to get across in class. His lecture therefore comes across as well organized, thorough, and spiced with examples that make students want to learn.

Highet suggests that teachers should "brisken up the course. Bring in novel illustrations. Read controversial discussion of problems in the subject" (*The Art of Teaching*). "The outline provides the foundation and struts of the lecture, but new material gives it a fresh coat of paint" (ibid.).

The flexible lecture has the advantage of giving continuity to a course because students in one semester are getting basically the same subject matter as those who took the class before them. But the outline allows the easy addition or deletion of new material, especially on a word processor. A teacher can call up the outline on the computer and add new material with ease. Classroom preparation is one of the surest guarantees for a well-taught course. A class that works is usually the result of a teacher who has planned well. If the subject matter is new and intricate, preparation insures a teacher's command of the material and her ability to communicate it with authority and accuracy.

The Perils of Nonpreparation

Peter Abelard was known as one of the best teachers in the twelfth century, but he had a problem. He fell in love with one of his students—the bright and beautiful Heloise. The romance between Abelard and Heloise is well known, but not so the impact of the infatuation on Abelard's teaching. Abelard described what happened: "In measure as this passionate rapture absorbed me more and more, I devoted ever less time to philosophy and to the work of the school. Indeed it became loathsome to me to go to the school or to linger there; the labour, moreover, was very burdensome, since my nights were vigils of love and my days of study. My lecturing became utterly careless and lukewarm; I did nothing because of inspiration, but everything merely as a matter of habit. I had become nothing more than a reciter of my former secrets of philosophy" (Smith, et al., *Lives in Education*, 75–76).

Abelard's students let him know his teaching had declined. He wrote: "As for the sorrow, the groans, the lamentations of my students when they perceived the preoccupation, nay, rather the chaos, of my mind, it is hard to even imagine them" (ibid.). Most teachers don't have the same problem as Abelard, but it's easy to slip into the habit of not preparing classes. An instructor reasons that he has covered the material so many times before that a five minute review before class time is all he needs. But anyone who has taught for awhile knows that such is a game of "instructional roulette." A quick review and an alert mind occasionally produces a good class, but most often a lack of preparation shows. The material is often disorganized, the key ideas are fuzzy and the examples are stale. Preparation is like a good insurance policy: you're not always aware of it, but it provides great protection when you need it.

THE DIALECTIC

If Plato had a hard time keeping the attention of students, Socrates had no trouble at all. Socrates prodded and cajoled his charges into looking at many sides of a subject. One of his favorite methods of teaching was the dialectic. The dialectic worked for Socrates and it works for many teachers today because students have to do more than listen and digest information. They think and learn better if they're actively involved. The dialectic invites participation.

Many believe the dialectic is simply a process of questions and answers. But it's more than that. Socrates saw the dialectic as a clash of ideas, a mental joust that produced insights for the participants. Socrates started with a statement: "Persuasion in Athens is more concerned with gaining power than finding truth." He would then encourage students to argue the opposite of what he had said. His statement was considered the thesis and the students' reaction was called the antithesis. Through the give-and-take of lively agreement or disagreement, students and teacher arrived at the "synthesis." or a combination of the best thinking from the thesis and the antithesis.

An instructor wants her students to understand the reasons for the Protestant Reformation. She might begin by stating that Luther was wrong to rebel against the pope, and that he should have worked within the Catholic Church for reform. Then she would encourage students to critically evaluate her ideas. Some might argue that reform within the Church would have been impossible given the turmoil of the times. The only way Luther could have made his point was to break away. One student might support his claim by showing that reformers like Savonarola had tried, but weren't successful. Then the teacher might respond by saying that Luther had great persuasive skills, which he could have used to get a hearing and still stay a faithful son of the Church. The student would respond by emphasizing that many Church leaders were not ready to take advice from a monk. The clash of ideas in a spirit of critical inquiry gets students to examine the validity of their ideas and to come up with new insights. To work, the teacher needs to explain what she is doing and why. Some students are reluctant to take on the instructor in what appears to be an argument. Some teachers don't like any kind of conflict, even on the idea level. A well-planned dialectic works in two ways: it gets students involved and it helps them see all sides of a question. It shouldn't be used all the time. Just as a steady diet of steak would become wearisome after a while, a constant use of the dialectic would wear a class down. But applied occasionally for good reason, the dialectic is an effective teaching tool.

Questions

Closely linked to the dialectic is the question. Like a Swiss army knife, a question can serve a number of purposes. It can seek information, act as a catalyst for discussion and get students involved better than a statement.

Questions can deal with fact, interpretation or opinion. A high-school teacher is covering J. D. Salinger's *Catcher in the Rye*. She can ask something simple, like "Who wrote the book?" Or, "What is the name of the main character?" She can then move on and ask an interpretive question, "Is Salinger simply telling the story about a troubled adolescent, or is he trying to communicate a message?" She can probe further and ask, "Do you think Holden Caufield is typical of adolescents in the 2000s, even though Salinger wrote in the 1950s?"

Good questions take planning. That's why many teachers write out a series of questions before class. Then they either write the questions on the board as a stimulant to thought or they sprinkle them throughout the lecture to keep interest.

The Joy of Teaching

Who Should Answer Questions?

Students can be divided into many categories, but most teachers know that a typical class includes those who want to answer every question, ones who volunteer occasionally, and a few who would like it just fine if they never had to answer. If an instructor asks a question, she can always rely on a faithful few to answer. She also knows that a few won't respond unless she prods them. Most good instructors call on those who want to answer questions, but they also ask the reluctant because then everyone gets involved. If all students in a class know that their turn could come at any time, they're more motivated to study the material in advance and to listen during the class period. Thomas Kasaulis states "For a question to be effective, it must ask about the right issue, at the right time, of the right persons" (taken from chapter 4, "Questioning," in Margaret Morganroth Gullette, ed., *The Art and Craft of Teaching*, 42). Thus, framing questions can be as important as structuring a lecture.

Master teachers often get students to think about each other's answers. A political-science teacher might ask, "Was the Johnson administration correct in ordering the bombing of Haiphong harbor during the Vietnam conflict?" One student might say, "Yes, because the United States needed to send a message." The instructor could then ask another student what he thought of the first student's comment. In this kind of question, the teacher is not trying to get the "correct" answer but to stimulate discussion and to get students to think about an issue.

If the discussion gets heated, so much the better. Students tend to remember material they feel strongly about. Even those students who sit passively by and listen can usually gain something from a spirited exchange.

Getting students involved

One of the secrets of good teaching is variety. Instructors who always follow the same method—lecture, dialectic, reading from the book—are bound to bore. The best teachers use a mix depending on the subject matter, the time of day or semester and the students. They keep a class moving and apply the method that works best. They also make sure students get involved.

Some students resist in-class activities, but most enjoy getting involved if the exercises are well designed and reinforce the material taught.

Over the years, I've picked up a number of useful exercises designed to demonstrate how difficult it is to listen during a conversation. To use the exercise, divide the class into triads. Two of the three will talk on opposite sides of a controversial topic and the third keeps time and observes. Give students a list of pro and con subjects—capital punishment, abortion, tighter restrictions on handguns, banning of smoking, etc. Then tell students to pick a side and prepare a one-minute argument promoting their position. One student argues that smoking should be completely banned from public places, and the other defends a smoker's right to puff in certain areas. Divide the class into quartets if the numbers don't allow triads. Two can observe and time. Each student has about four minutes to prepare one argument on his or her side of the issue. Then with the other student observing, student one presents the single argument for one minute with the person on the opposite side listening. At the end of the minute, the third student calls time. The student who has been listening has to repeat or at least paraphrase what the first person said. When this has been accomplished to the satisfaction of the first student, the second presents her point of view.

The exercise demonstrates the difficulty of both really listening to what someone else is saying and preparing a response. Humans can both listen and think of a response because the mind travels four times faster than the voice. But most people think about what they're going to say rather than listening to what the other person says. When the topic is controversial, the challenge is even greater.

After the exercise, a teacher can ask the two talking participants how hard they found it to listen. She can ask the timekeeper/observer to comment on how well the two communicated.

TEXTBOOKS

At one time or another, most teachers have picked a text in haste and lived to regret their decision. Selecting a good text is like hiring the right employee for a job. Some applicants look perfect at first glance, but turn out to be disasters once they start working. Certain texts appear just right during a quick reading of the table of contents. But once used in class, it becomes painfully obvious that the book is not right for the course. Then the teacher has the sticky job of trying to get students to read a text he doesn't like himself.

Some teachers make the text a major part of the course. Others almost never use it. Most instructors fall between the two extremes. The text isn't the heart of the course but helps reinforce the material learned. Like the rudder of a well-steered ship, the text provides direction. It also gives students something they can see, feel and read. An excellent text won't save a sinking class, but a bad one won't ruin an otherwise well taught course.

Guidelines for picking a text include (1) Does it clearly illustrate and supplement the material being taught in class? (2) Is it readable and interesting? (3) Does it give students something they can refer to if they don't understand what was covered in class?

Some texts are academically solid, interesting, and just right for the course. Others are dry and dull as dust. Teachers will obviously get more mileage from the former kind. For that reason, it's well worth the time and effort to search out and choose the right text.

Getting Students to Read the Text

Presuming you have a good text, how do you get students to read it? Weimer interviewed numerous colleagues about the frustrating problem of students who don't read the text. She states: "Many students do not read, period—not for pleasure, not for information, not for inspiration" (*The Teaching Professor*, vol. 3, 4, p. 1). Some teachers use the pop quiz to stimulate reading and this works to a degree. But Weimer emphasizes that the "stick" isn't as effective as the "carrot" because the sudden quiz is an extrinsic motivator. It can also induce hostile feelings in students because many of them hate surprises, even though they know they should have read the material. Weimer suggests some better and more intrinsic methods:

1. Give students reasons to read. Tell them why you're assigning a text and explain how it fits into the course.//
2. Talk about the assigned material in class and show how it relates. Open the book to a specific page and discuss the key ideas you find.
3. Assume students have read the material and run the class accordingly. Don't ask how many have read the assignment.

4. Enjoy and value the reading yourself and let students know it (ibid., 1–2).

Another approach is to ask students about the assigned reading on a daily basis. Students then get the clear message that the text is an important supplement to the lecture/discussion. If one student hasn't read the material, move on to someone else. Berating the nonreader in front of the class usually forces the student to focus on the humiliation of being dressed down. For most young people, not knowing the answer in the presence of one's peers is humiliating enough.

Repetition

The Jesuits have a saying "Repetitio est mater studiorum" ("Repetition is the mother of study"). Most teachers routinely review material they've taught. Such a review can range from something brief at the end of each class period to a comprehensive run-through near the end of the term. Reviews yield a number of benefits. Many students don't grasp a concept the first time it's presented, even though they pretend they do. Few students will raise their hand and say, "I didn't get that. Would you go over it again?" Even students who understand material the first time through quickly forget unless the teacher reexplains and reinforces key points.

Before I went back to graduate school, I attended a three-day seminar sponsored by Purdue University. The workshop was entitled "How to Survive in College," and it offered a number of practical tips on how to study better. One principle in particular was reassuring; the only difference between a genius and the rest of us is that we may not understand a concept as quickly as a genius, but if we keep trying, we can grasp it just as well. Presuming a student has average or above average intelligence, he can understand calculus if he's patient and takes the time to let the concepts sink in. Once he understands concepts, he knows them as well as someone in Mensa—the club that limits its membership to people with IQs of at least 150. Most teachers recognize that some of the students in a class will understand material after the first explanation, others will pick it up on the third or fourth go-around and some will need to come in for extra help after class. This staggered learning process makes repetition all the more worthwhile. An instructor can drill material into the ground and bore some of the brighter students with too many explanations, but most students are glad to hear principles covered again because it gives them the security of realizing they know it well.

Many colleges require a comprehensive exam for majors. Students often react to the experience with dread because they fear they can't pull together the material from all their major classes and express themselves coherently to the examining professors. But once they start studying the classes, they not only review what they've learned, but they gain new insights. They also see how the courses fit together and often reinforce each other. Many a student will comment that the review was one of their best learning experiences.

COMPUTERS

Mike Hazel has taught at both the high school and college levels and has adapted the benefits of using computers in the classroom. The computer is a powerful teaching tool. Anyone who has made the leap from writing on a typewriter to composing on a word processor knows what a friend the machine is. Computers will never replace teachers, but they can make teaching easier and more effective. Children can learn math and enjoy rather than endure the experience. Students can write better and faster. Teachers have at their fingertips mounds of information, which they can draw up with a push of a button. Many teachers are afraid of using computers either because they believe the computer might somehow replace them or they're not quite sure how to use it effectively. But once mastered, computers make teaching better and more pleasant for everyone.

A high school in North Dakota was able to equip its entire school with computers. The difference in student learning was dramatic. Seniors wrote their term papers on word processors instead of grinding them out long hand or on typewriters. Before, their papers were ten to twelve pages. With the word processors, they were spinning out twenty-five page essays that were not only longer but better written.

With the touch of a few buttons, students can quickly learn to move paragraphs around, delete sentences that are too wordy and polish a piece of writing until it glows.

In the twenty-first century, many undergraduate and graduate university classes are being delivered entirely on the computer via the Internet. This recent innovation has generated resistance among some teachers who favor more traditional modes of instruction, but online learning is here to stay because of the student demand for learning, despite geographical limitations and work and family obligations. In addition, many students are more willing to disclose interpersonal information via online communication than in face to face classroom situations. Online communication, because of its reliance on writing, also requires students to be more careful and purposeful in how they craft messages. The communication dynamic that emerges from this new approach leads to excellent discussions and innovative and exciting new approaches for teaching and learning.

Most teachers can recount stories of movie projectors that wouldn't work, electrical cords that broke thirty seconds before class and viewgraphs with letters so small no one could read them. Such incidents entertained students, but also made many a teacher vow to swear off anything electronic. Audiovisuals seem easy to use, but they're not. It takes coordination to turn on the switch, pull out the viewgraph, put it in the right position on the overhead and talk at the same time. One slip can throw any teacher off stride. A class can be torpedoed by a viewgraph that appears upside down or an overhead projector that make letters look like the bottom line of an optometrist's chart. But with a little practice, teachers can blend audio-visuals into their classes and feel comfortable with the process.

Most students learn best when they use their minds and senses. Ten slides of Dublin help illustrate a lecture on Irish history better than a half hour of narration by itself

History professor Giovanni Costigan was an eloquent spellbinder who was once asked whether he used visual aids. He responded, "I am the visual aid." Costigan was really a humble man who was telling the truth.

Most teachers can't make Costigan's claim. They know that a combination of showing and telling is often the best way to explain subject matter. Few educators can go into a classroom and keep students enthralled for an hour. A whiteboard not only makes material clearer, but students learn better because they combine seeing with hearing.

Like anything else, audiovisuals become easy through continuous use. When they work and an instructor knows how to use them well, audiovisuals are superb teaching aids and are well worth the time it takes to blend them into a lecture or discussion.

While the above-mentioned visual aids are simple and effective, with the development and increased presence of computers in classrooms and dorm rooms, many professors (as well as students) employ PowerPoint as means to enhance their presentations and lectures. PowerPoint slides are simple to make on the computer and allow for very interesting innovations to presentations. Visual imagery can be more easily added into lectures and speeches. Even Internet links to video and audio clips can be easily embedded into slides, leading to far more interesting and innovative classroom presentations.

A more recent innovation is the use of a hybrid approach to teaching, where online "Blackboard" Web sites are created to augment a traditional classroom experience. These Web sites allow for discussion forums, course resources, and even class lectures to be available for the students. As our computer use continues to increase, this hybrid approach to teaching will invariably become a more popular innovation for teachers delivering a variety of subjects.

5

Polishing Speaking Skills

> "Teachers share with other speakers a fundamental reliance on an ability to engage an audience and to stimulate emotions."
>
> —Joseph Lowman

WHEN I WAS IN the second grade, I had to give a book report to the entire school. The book was *The Arabian Nights*, and my mother spent two days sewing an outfit that looked very Arabian. I should have spent as much time preparing the report.

When I walked out and faced all those students, from fellow classmates to smirking eighth graders, I lost it. I couldn't utter a word. That moment is frozen in my brain as one of the most humiliating of my life. I remember my compassionate second-grade teacher ending the ordeal by nudging me off stage.

Most teacher-education programs include some training in speaking skills, but curricula often focus more on lesson plans, teaching methods and educational philosophy than on public speaking. So many teachers walk into their first classroom lugging the same anxieties as any other human who doesn't like talking in front of a group.

An effective teacher doesn't have to be a dynamic platform orator, but it helps. Outstanding instructors project energy, deep concern about their subject, and strong delivery. Most teachers concede that speaking ability is essential for successful teaching. To speak well in front of a class, instructors need to channel nervousness, be well prepared, and use their voice like an actress or actor. Lowman emphasizes that "college classrooms are fundamentally dramatic arenas in which the teacher is the focal point, just as the actor or orator is on a stage" (*Mastering the Techniques of Teaching*, 11). The same principle applies to primary and secondary classrooms.

Often public speaking means the difference between a teacher who is competent and one who is outstanding.

TAMING SPEECH FRIGHT

Stage or "speech fright" is something most people have experienced at least once, and the bad memories still linger. Teachers don't get a reprieve from fear because they're members of a profession that requires public speaking skills. Stage fright is usually a problem for the new teacher—and sometimes remains so for seasoned veterans. A number of reasons account for this unpleasant feeling: fear of the unknown, fear of failure, and a lack of preparation. In a normal conversation, one person can take a breather while the other picks up the slack. But in a public setting, a solo speaker has to command an audience's attention and keep it over a period of time. This takes practice and most people don't deliver speeches very often.

Speech fright can be a nightmare or a blessing, depending on how a speaker handles it. If a teacher practices a few easy techniques and knows the material well, stage fright turns from a bane to a benefit. Famous actors and speakers admit they still get butterflies after many years of performing. But most emphasize that nervousness gives them an edge because it makes them more dynamic.

THE POSITIVE SIDE OF SPEECH FRIGHT

One of the most comforting phenomena for an uptight speaker is the "energizer effect." A combination of three elements helps rather than hurts a speaker: nervousness, an audience and thorough preparation. A teacher who is nervous but who has prepared carefully finds that her mind becomes more alert as a result of the preparation and the added challenge of an audience. The stage fright energizes the mind and helps it remember better. The opposite happens if the speaker is nervous but hasn't prepared. Then the material gets distorted as the speaker gropes for an idea in front of an expectant audience. The moral is: don't worry about being nervous because speech fright is a plus for the prepared speaker. Be concerned only about not being prepared.

Polishing Speaking Skills

THE JOY OF SPEAKING

When done well, speaking in front of an audience can be exhilarating. A lively lecture to students, an articulate talk to fellow faculty, or a carefully crafted presentation to the school board is a pleasure for speaker and audience. Most teachers can recall classes when everything clicked. They knew their material, expressed it with precision and flair, and students responded with excitement. Like other skills, speaking well doesn't happen by chance. Most, if not all, outstanding speakers have sharpened their eloquence over the years. Jack Anderson, the Washington, DC columnist, was an excellent public speaker. I remember a few years ago he came to Gonzaga University and gave a lecture on Watergate, the ill-fated Republican break-in of the Watergate apartment complex. Anderson stood before his audience of college students and recalled with eloquence the unfolding events of Watergate.

On the way to the airport the next morning, I asked him how he learned to speak so well. He responded that he sharpened his skills as a Mormon missionary in the South. Day after day, he gave talks, and the practice paid off.

Very few speakers can deliver a good impromptu talk. In a speech tournament, an impromptu speech is one in which the contestant is given a topic and has seconds to prepare. Many so-called impromptu talks have been given many times. Most of us can recall an occasion, perhaps at a sports banquet, where the master of ceremonies asked a coach—usually someone named Rocky or Biff—to get up and say a few words to the assembled athletes. Rocky rose from the fifth table, near the podium, muscled his way to the microphone, and delivered an inspiring fifteen-minute oration on "team spirit and the need to keep playing until the final gun." Rocky has given the speech over one-hundred times during his coaching career and lives for the next banquet.

A speaker who doesn't prepare is playing rhetorical roulette. If he's on, he may be able to deliver coherent thoughts with little preparation. But he's taking a big chance. If he's in front of an audience, is nervous but hasn't prepared, his mind can go blank or get jammed. Jamming occurs when the speaker is aware that he's not coherent and is worrying about the impression he's making. He's thinking, "I've gone blank. I don't like this feeling and I wish all those people out there would stop staring at me." He finds it hard to think such thoughts and at the same time to remember what he wanted to say to his audience. Following are some preparation techniques the pros use.

Organization

Unless you're giving a commencement address at Harvard or a talk to the United Nations, you'll find it more useful to speak from an outline rather than a word-for-word manuscript. A memorized speech is fine for those occasions where the speaker wants precise wording. But for most situations, teachers will get more mileage from an outline rather than a word-for-word script. The outline format does not have o be rigid.

Professional speakers favor the outline because it gives them more control and a better chance to maintain eye contact with their audience. Senator John Danforth of Missouri says: "The vast majority of my speeches are extemporaneous. I have found that the quality of my extemporaneous speeches is in inverse proportion to the length of my notes. When my notes are too elaborate, I tend to rely too much on deciphering what I have jotted down, and too little on putting my message across to the audience. Therefore, the best approach for me is to write out three to six Roman numerated points, each with maybe three sub points" (quoted in Hanna et al., *Public Speaking for Personal Sucess*). Outlines come in a variety of formats: topical, story, complication/development/resolution, cause and effect. An outline doesn't have to be long and elaborate, especially if a teacher already knows the subject matter well.

The Big-Box, Little-Box Approach

One useful outlining technique is the "Big Box, Little Box Format." Dominic LaRusso taught this method for years at the University of Washington. Think of a lecture-discussion as one big box. Within the big box are three smaller boxes—an introduction, a body, and a conclusion. Each of the boxes can be broken down further. See illustration below. (Leave space for illustration.)

The following visual is a way to illustrate how an outline divides a speech into manageable parts. The approach is like looking at a scene through a telescope, with the naked eye, and through a microscope. The first look gives an overview. The second gets closer, and the third closer yet.

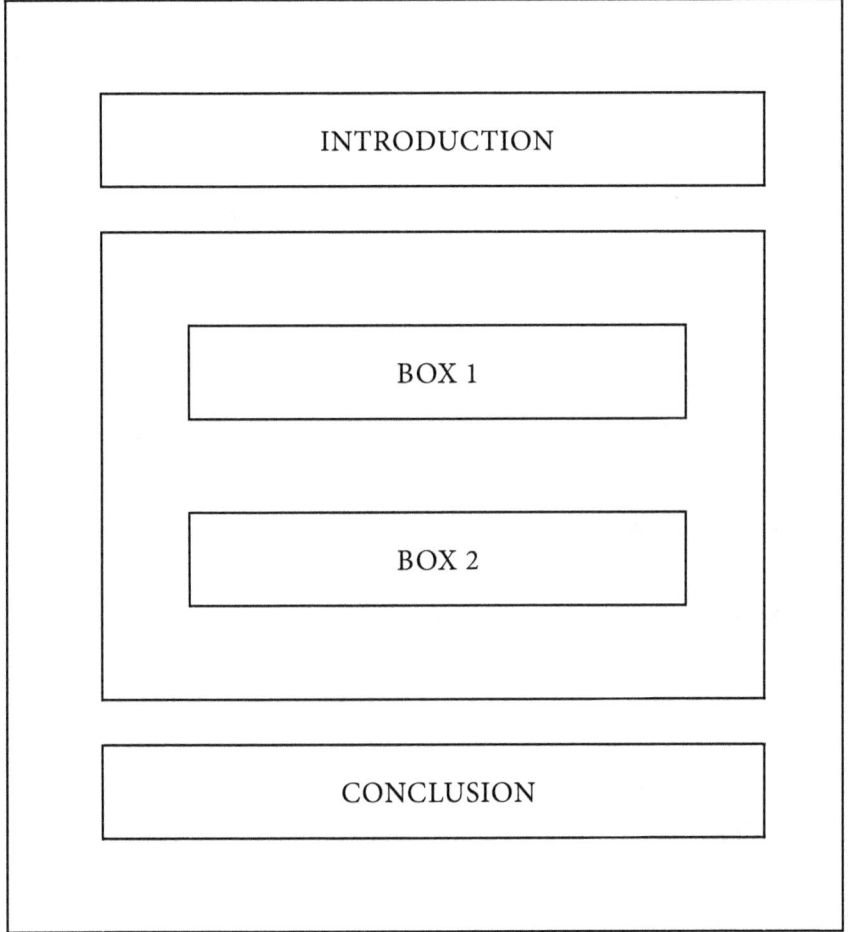

FIGURE 2: Big Box, Little Box

The thesis sentence is the glue that holds the outline together. English teachers have been promoting the thesis sentence since the third grade, but most students haven't realized its value. The thesis sentence gives order and unity to a lecture, speech or essay. If I were giving a lecture on the material from this chapter, my thesis sentence might be "Speaking is fearful for many, but it can be tamed with effective organization and delivery." The sentence covers what I want to say and controls any research I will do. If the material I look up doesn't fit the thesis sentence, I don't use it. Armed with the thesis sentence, a speaker can construct a one page outline based on everything she already knows about the topic. Let's say parents in a small community have protested sophomores studying J. D. Salinger's *Catcher in the Rye* because of the language and sexual innuendos. The school principal asks the teacher who uses the book in her course to justify it in a speech to parents at a PTA meeting. The instructor knows the topic well, but she's not sure how to organize what she knows. So she jots down a thesis statement like, "Despite its sometimes-graphic language and references to sexuality during adolescence, *Catcher in the Rye* is well written and is especially strong in showing what it's like to be a teenager." Under her thesis sentence, she might write:

I. The book is well written and is a good model for aspiring writers.

II. *Catcher* gives an accurate and perceptive picture of what it's like to be a teenager.

But then she realizes that concerned parents won't be interested in such information until she allays their fears about the sexual language. So she revises and her first outline looks like this:

I. Objections to the book

    A. Language

    B. Sexuality in adolescence

    C. Answer to each

II. Benefits to studying *Catcher in the Rye*

    A. The book is well written and is a model for young writers.

    B. The character of Holden Caulfied helps paint a realistic picture of the teenage years.

Under each of the major boxes or headings, she can put down whatever she already knows about the book. She can then start doing her research. She might look up magazine articles about school districts that have had similar reactions to the book. She may pull out sections of the novel to illustrate that the language is realistic and is not unusual for an adolescent. She might read reviews of the book. She may revise her outline headings as she does research, but the outline has given her a structure.

An outline with a thesis sentence followed by two or three major categories gives the speech the order it needs—much like the foundation and frame of a house. Without the foundation and the frame, the rest of the house can't stand—or if it does for a while, it can fall into a heap.

An introduction comes first during the delivery of a talk, but most speakers prepare their grabber after the body of the speech is finished. Why? The introduction has at least two purposes: to grab the attention of the audience and to establish rapport with them. But the speaker doesn't have a good idea of what would be a good attention-getter unless she has developed the body of the talk first. The attention-getter might be a quotation, a story or a simple statement of welcome in the case of parents coming to the talk about justifying *Catcher in the Rye*.

Most speakers compose their conclusion last. The conclusion is primarily a summary of key points plus a sentence that ties the talk together. Much like reporters on a news program, speakers construct a final sentence that summarizes and leaves something striking in the minds of listeners. For the Catcher speech, a summary statement might look like: "I appreciate this chance to explain why we're teaching *Catcher in the Rye*. We believe the book is well written and gives an excellent portrait of a young man struggling through adolescence. In this case, art imitates reality and students who read the book have a better understanding of what it means to be fifteen years old. They'll also have studied some first-rate writing."

As a general rule, the better the speaker knows the topic, the simpler the outline. If the subject is complicated, a longer outline will give more control. The topic "How to sign your children up for sports this fall," is easier than "How to interpret our school's sexual harassment policy."

The Joy of Teaching

The Velcro Approach to Memory and Imagination

A memorized speech is like Teflon—it doesn't stick easily. The word-for-word manuscript is time consuming and hard to deliver. The speaker is tied to words rather than ideas. The combination of a flexible outline and use of vivid imagination is like Velcro. Images grafted in the mind stay there.

Experienced speakers resort to a memorized manuscript if the occasion is solemn and they want to use exact and elegant language. But most of the time, the well-arranged and vividly imagined outline works better.

A teacher can remember a movie she saw in the third grade but can't recall the subject of yesterday's faculty meeting. The movie had some impact on her life, and she's probably recalled it often over the years. If she saw *The Wizard of Oz* when she was eight, twelve, and twenty-one, the pictures of Dorothy and her three friends are deeply embedded in her memory. But yesterday's meeting may not have held strong interest for her, and it dealt with abstract ideas that were hard to remember. If an experience is vivid, repeated and linked to something else that's important in our lives, we'll remember it. If it's theoretical, unimportant, and recalled only once or twice, it disappears.

Books on improving memory have been around since ancient Greece. Most emphasize three ways to rivet material in the mind: association, imagination, and repetition. A speaker remembers ideas that are linked together, vividly imagined, and repeated. To try this principle, take ten items that have no connection to one other. Let's say the items are the movie character ET, a pine tree, blue suede shoes, a telephone pole, stairs, broken glass, a brick, a yellow Volkswagen, an angry librarian, and a cup of coffee. If we try to recall the items as separate chunks, it's hard to remember them all. Instead of seeing the items as separate, imagine ET driving up to a library in a yellow Volkswagen. A brick rests on the passenger seat of the VW. He parks between a pine tree and a telephone pole, grabs the brick and steps out. After walking up the stairs of the library, he hurls the brick through the glass door. The brick hits a cup of coffee the librarian is holding and splatters all over his blue suede shoes. The librarian gets mad, picks up the brick and throws it back at ET who is running down the stairs strewn with broken glass. ET leaps into his VW—parked between a pine tree and telephone pole—and roars away.

Polishing Speaking Skills

If you vividly imagined each item and went through a sequence of putting them together, you could recall them all rather easily. If you repeated the sequence a few times, you would have the series locked in your mind.

You can easily apply the same principle to the outline. Form a vivid image for each of the major points of the presentation. Let's say the teacher giving the talk on *Catcher in the Rye* wants to begin with a story of a student named Greg whom she knew ten years ago. Greg is a surgeon now but had a rocky time as a sophomore in her English class. Greg strongly reminds her of Holden Caulfield. The student, like Holden, is groping for a sense of identity in a world he doesn't understand. The teacher vividly fixes in her mind a picture of Greg and what he did. She sees his face, imagines the way he talked and goes through the steps she wanted to use in her story. She then vividly imagines the parts of the thesis sentence. She does the same for all the major categories.

She then links all the parts together. The opening story leads to the thesis statement. The thesis statement is hooked to the first major point of the body and so on until the conclusion. The speaker relies on a series of images rather than sentences.

To reinforce each of the images, she marks key words with a yellow highlighter. Then, she draws a picture of each major idea in the introduction, body and conclusion. Artistic ability doesn't count here: stick figures or pictures that would fail in a second grade art class will do just fine. The point is to fuse the mental with the visual. Using this approach, the *Catcher in the Rye* outline would like this:

Grabber: Tell audience you're glad they're here and you're happy to discuss an important topic. Then tell story of Greg.

   I. Objections to the book

    A. Language

    B. Sexuality in adolescence

        1. Example of Greg and Tina

        2. Link to the book

    C. Answer to each:

        1. Language

        2. Sexuality

II. Benefits of studying *Catcher*
   A. Well written and model for young writers
      1. Read passage from p. 2
      2. Show why this is good writing
   B. Holden paints realistic picture and is someone sophomores can relate to
      1. Describe Holden's qualities
      2. Show how Holden is like many fifteen-year-olds today

Conclusion: Thanks for listening.

Summarize key points

Final sentence

I would be happy to answer any questions you have

The speaker can glance at the outline during the talk and the highlighted words and drawings will stand out. She doesn't have to read each of the sentences because the key words or pictures reinforce a vividly imagined idea. The AIR (Association / Imagination / Repetition) formula allows the speaker freedom to concentrate on the audience and the ideas. If she doesn't follow her outline exactly, no one in the audience knows it.

Like other human skills, the memory method works best with practice. To make the technique a habit, concoct a vivid image for every idea. If you see in your mind the character Caliban, the dark monster in Shakespeare's *The Tempest*, you'll remember him much better. It doesn't matter that Shakespeare's original image doesn't conform to your picture. What's important is to graft a vivid image in the mind for instant recall later.

A teacher can apply the AIR method in two ways: she can remember the main ideas of the speech and she can imagine the setting in advance. She can see herself confidently walking into the PTA meeting, staying in complete control throughout and delivering a well prepared talk. If she's in the habit of using the meditation and guided imagery approach discussed in Chapter 2, the speech becomes another "interesting challenge" to be met during the day. During her quiet time, she envisions the speech, the audience and the key ideas she wants to get across.

Polishing Speaking Skills

The Importance of the First Thirty Seconds

The phrase "You never get a second chance to make a good first impression" applies in public speaking. The first thirty seconds are crucial in forging a bond between speaker and audience. If a speaker mumbles, fiddles with the microphone and asks "Is this thing working?" his opener is about as appetizing as last week's coffee. But if he walks to center stage with a brisk confidence, a smile and an opening comment about how glad he is to be with the audience, he's set a positive tone that should carry him through the whole talk.

Like other human relationships, the bond between speaker and audience thrives on liking and respect. Top presenters brim with assurance and warmth. They telegraph the message verbally and nonverbally "I like you. I'm glad to be here and I have something important I want to share with you." Professionals also use a device that helps them establish an immediate rapport and helps carry them throughout the talk. As they start to speak, they look at those audience members who are smiling. Such folks can be friends or benevolent strangers. Good speakers carry on a conversation with the friendly members until they're into their rhythm. Then they look at the nonsmilers and address them.

It's rare that an audience has no one who is friendly, but it happens. What to do then? Imagine someone you know who really likes you and rivet the person's smiling face in your mind. Talk to the friend for a minute or two and then focus on your live audience. Most speakers affirm that the first minute or two is the hardest and once they get into a talk, what was a chore turns into a pleasant and invigorating experience. Throughout the presentation, keep telling yourself that you really like this audience and they'll respond in kind. Enjoy the challenge of sharing well prepared thoughts.

How to Improve Your Voice

Voice consultant Dorothy Sarnoff (*Speech Can Change Your Life*) has spent years helping people polish their delivery. Ms. Sarnoff confirms what most of us know but don't pay much attention to: we really don't know how our voice sounds, but everybody else does. Two minutes of listening to a tape recording of our voice will convince most of us that we need some work. The voice is the primary reflection of personality and is one of a teacher's major tools in communicating to students. Like a musical instrument, the voice can delight or turn off listeners. How it sounds has a strong impact on students.

Most of us can recall a teacher who walked into the classroom on the first day looking handsome and well dressed. As soon as he opened his mouth, the class winced. His voice hovered somewhere between running a finger down a blackboard and the screeching of a microphone that hasn't been properly tuned. Most of us can also recall teachers whose pleasant, firm voices made them appealing and effective, even though they didn't have a striking physical appearance.

To get a notion of how students hear you, record your voice during the next conversation or class and then sit back and listen. Assume you've never heard this person before. Would you describe the sound as pleasant, neutral or grating? Was it dull and flat or full and clear? Did you talk too fast and mangle some of your syllables? Would you want to listen to yourself for fifty minutes? Very few people—including the best teachers—like their voice when they hear it recorded. Most are surprised by the way they sound. But the voice they hear is the one that everyone else gets. Some people react to a recording by making a vow of perpetual silence. Others shrug and say, "Well, that's me. If people don't like it, too bad." Most conclude that they need to do something about the unpleasant aspects of their voice but really never get around to a program that will produce change.

After listening to a recording of your voice, focus on what you find attractive about the way you sound. Like students, most teachers get discouraged if they concentrate only on the negative. Build on your strengths and trim the flaws. Your vocal sound might be pleasant but the rate is too fast. The inflection is lively but some of the syllables get lost in a mumble.

Five elements make up vocal sound: projection, pitch, inflection, rate, and articulation. Most successful teachers exude energy, variety, and resonance. They speak slowly enough to be understood and enunciate their words so listeners don't have to strain to catch what they're saying.

Projection

When I was an undergraduate, I took a speech course from an instructor named Art Quine. Art was like no other teacher. As a young man, he hated giving speeches because he had a slight vocal impediment. But he overcame his fear of the platform and organized his own class around the

Polishing Speaking Skills

principle of projection. He maintained that speakers could make their nervousness a blessing instead of a curse if they would project their voices. Most people naturally do two things that make public speaking harder: they speak faster and softer than they do in normal conversation. Art had his students deliver what he called the "fanatic speaker" talk. He told each of us to take a controversial position—i.e., cut down the redwoods, ban birthdays, build a monument to Fidel Castro. We then advocated our position to an audience instructed to boo and hiss when Art gave them the signal. He stood behind the speaker and let him deliver a line or two: "Despite what you've heard, redwoods are some of the ugliest trees in the world and should be destroyed." Art then raised his right hand and the audience booed and hissed. Art also appointed four hecklers in the front row and told them to make derogatory comments to the speaker. The orator then shouted over the taunts of his peers and hammered home points to the unreceptive audience. The key to survival was voice projection. If you spoke with energy and volume, you didn't feel nervousness. The exercise was fun and informative because it reinforced Art's point that vocal energy is salvation for the uptight.

As someone speaks, the air leaves the lungs on its way up the bronchial tubes, and then it strikes the vocal bands in the larynx. If a speaker is nervous and speaks softly, he can feel the tension. But if he projects, the tension disappears.

Speakers rarely have to shout at a hostile crowd. But the fanatic speech exercise confirmed that projection is one of the best cures for speech fright. Vocal projection makes most teachers more interesting to hear and gives them the sound of authority.

INFLECTION

Dominic LaRusso could spellbind an audience of five hundred or a class of twenty-two. Much of his dynamism came from a voice that was resonant and varied. He could move his audience by shifting his inflection. Most great speakers do the same. None of them speak in a monotone.

Pitch includes two elements: the high or low sound of the voice and the variety a speaker uses. If you have short, thin vocal bands, your voice will be high. Trying to speak deep and low with thin vocal bands is like trying to get a flute to sound like a trombone. Forcing the voice to a lower level than it can handle can also cause strain on the chords. Don Knotts will never sound like James Earl Jones because he doesn't have the same equipment.

Everyone has an "optimal pitch" range, which is the highest and lowest level a speaker can reach. But most don't take advantage of the range and many speak in a monotone without realizing how they sound.

If you want to improve inflection, listen to your voice on a tape recorder. Does it have plenty of variety? Do you sound lively? Would you be inspired to listen to yourself for more than five minutes? If the answers to those questions are "no," practice on the recorder and speak with much greater vocal variety than you're used to. Recite Shakespeare out loud and ham it up. Read a newspaper or book like a proclamation. Put much more inflection in the syllables than you really need to. If you're worried that family members or neighbors might think you've gone over the edge, record in the laundry room where no one can hear you. Experiment with your voice. As you listen to the playback, notice the difference in your vocal variety. You may not use the same inflection in class as you did when you recited Shakespeare in the basement, but your inflection should be more lively than it was before.

Study professionals and notice their inflection. Even their conversations are lively because of their vocal variety. They sound natural, but like most skills, the natural sounds come from practice.

Slowing Down a Rapid Rate

The famous motivational speaker Zig Ziglar admits that he speaks around 200 words per minute with "gusts" up to 400 words, but he knows the material so well that the speed seems natural to him. But for most teachers, a slower rate gives greater control and is easier for listeners to follow. If you can think at 400 words a minute, a 125 per minute speaking rate allows you to see in your mind the words you want to use. If you're talking at a clip of 200 words a minute, speech speed is getting closer to thought speed, and that makes it harder to think ahead to what you want to say. Like any other habit, rapid rate is hard to change. If you've been talking 150 words per minute for the last twenty years, it's hard to slow down to 115. But since you're speaking all the time in conversations, you have a great opportunity to practice a slower rate. Once you drop your speaking rate ten to fifteen words per minute, you'll be pleased at the greater control you have over what you're saying.

Slower Does Not Mean Duller

Most polished public speakers speak slower than the average conversationalist, but their voices brim with animation. In 1951, President Truman relieved General Douglas MacArthur of his command in Korea. The general returned to the United States and delivered one of the most stirring speeches in American history. Titled "Old Soldiers Never Die," the talk riveted an entire nation. MacArthur spoke around 105 words per minute, but his voice was drenched with feeling.

Improving Resonance

A few years ago, a radio announcer in Colorado kept getting marriage proposals. His rich baritone voice was a magnet that drew a number of admirers who had never seen what he looked like. But the resonant voice belonged to a small, plain looking man. North American advertisers hammer home the theme that physical looks are the keys that will unlock the door to happiness in marriage and business. But they pay little attention to the power of the voice to attract and motivate. Voice quality or resonance is the pleasant or unpleasant sound a speaker makes. If your voice sounds too harsh, take heart—resonance is one of the easiest vocal elements to change. Resonance is what happens to the sound after the air from the lungs and bronchial tubes strikes the vocal bands in the larynx. A carefully crafted guitar will transmit the rich sounds of the strings. The vocal resonators will do the same for the sound produced in the larynx.

The three major resonators are the throat, mouth and nasal passage. If the sound goes straight from the vocal chords to the nasal passage, a speaker projects a brass-like nasal twang—one of this planet's more unpleasant sounds. If the sound travels mostly into the mouth because the speaker has a cold and the nasal passage is blocked, the sound is stuffy. Ideal resonance is a nice balance of all three resonators—throat, mouth and nasal passage. Like a quality amplifier, the sounds are rich and pleasant.

If you want to improve voice quality, begin by listening again to your voice on a tape recorder. Do you like the sound? If you don't, is it because the quality is tight or harsh?

Start by thinking of yourself with a voice that has a clear, pleasant sound. Vivid imaging is just as important in projecting a quality tone as it is in relaying an attractive appearance. Then think of your mouth, throat and nasal passages as a fine instrument like a guitar or first-rate stereo. Your resonators are much like the amplifiers of a good system. Let the sounds roll around. Open up your mouth and experiment with the tone you want. Now play back the recording. Is the sound richer than before? If you notice only a little improvement, don't give up. Keep working until you have a sound you like.

After recording in private, tape conversations and class sessions. You'll then hear how you really sound to others. Listen as if you were someone else. Did you like the sound of the voice? What would you change? If you were pleased with the rate but found you spoke in a monotone, work on vocal variety during the next conversation or class session. After a week, record the class again and see if you're satisfied with the improvements.

Don't get discouraged, because restructuring a voice pattern takes time. Habits are hard to change and improvement won't happen in a day. Rivet in your mind the benefits of the new, better sounding you. A vigorous, pleasant voice will make you a better communicator in and out of the classroom.

Besides working with a tape recorder, be more aware of how you speak during conversations. Since you talk all through the day, you have plenty of chances to work on one of the five elements you believe will make you better as a teacher.

Friends won't think you're phony if you slow down, turn up the projection, or enunciate words more distinctly. You'll come across as more lively in conversation, and you can apply the improvement to classroom delivery.

6

How to Take the Pain out of Writing for Teachers and Students

> "If you find that writing is hard, it's because it is. It's one of the hardest things that people do."
>
> —William Zinsser

SOME TEACHERS HAVE TO write a lot and others very little. But virtually all educators have to compose memos, letters, reports and papers. All of this takes time and drains energy. But if writing is hard, it can be made easier with some tested methods.

WHY IS WRITING HARD?

One Danish author lamented that he would rather dig ditches for eight hours than write for four. Many educators would second his statement.

Writing well is tough for two reasons: (1) many students were taught grammar but weren't shown how to write, and (2) teachers have to fight against an "academic" or "official" style that still plagues education as much as it does business and the legal world (Calkins, *The Art of Teaching Writing*, 13). Many American and Canadian students have gone through a system in which they learned grammar and syntax, but no one showed them the steps needed to write well. Some instructors taught their charges how to use the *Guide to Periodical Literature*, the mechanics of how to construct footnotes and a bibliography, plus the correct format for a term paper. But not every writing teacher took students from the first idea for an essay to a completed, polished manuscript. As a result, legions of students fear writing because they don't know how to do it.

Besides lack of training in the process of writing, many students learned along the way to write in a stuffy, abstract style. Students wrote clear, simple sentences in the first few grades. But around high school, they had to read textbooks with phrases like "systemic conceptualized framework" or "implement the socialization process." If the experts wrote like that, why shouldn't students?

English professor Joseph Williams did a survey and found that many high-school teachers promote abstract, pretentious writing. Instead of giving good grades to students who write clearly and concisely, instructors often reward what Williams calls a "heavy-handed, nominal" style. The nominal style features long words with Latin origins, rather than short, precise ones. An example of the nominal style is, "There was an investigation into the causes of the changes in the cell by the scientists." The more direct way is, "The scientists investigated why the cell changed" (Lauerman, "Teachers Can't Tell Good Prose from Bad").

The problem of abstract writing often got worse in college, especially in the large universities. Charles Sykes asks: "How is it that normally intelligent, occasionally articulate, sometimes even eloquent men and women become pompous, opaque, and incomprehensible the moment they enter academe" (*ProfScam*). (Sykes suggests that obscure language is a way to make the trivial sound impressive [ibid.].) In a professional article about television's *The A-Team*, one sentence reads: "The male group is ubiquitous in colonizing the conventional spheres of interpersonal activity as a self-sufficient autonomous unit." Translation: *The A-Team* is about a bunch of macho guys who hang around together doing macho things" (Sykes, *ProfScam*, 111).

It would be unfair to claim that all or most professors write in an abstract and murky manner, but the "academic style" is often proposed to high-school and college students as the model for their class assignments.

A SYSTEM TO TAKE THE PAIN OUT OF WRITING

So how can teachers make their own writing easier, clearer and more effective? How can they pass along these steps to their students? Following are some suggestions.

The first step is to ask, what one key idea do I want to get across in the memo, letter or report? The key idea or "thesis sentence" is the plumb line that gives unity to a piece of writing. Zinsser emphasizes, "I'll state as a rule of thumb that every successful piece of nonfiction should leave the reader with one provocative thought that he didn't have before. Not two thoughts, or five—just one" (Zinnsser, *On Writing Well*, 63).

For this chapter, the one thought I want to convey is that writing is hard, but it can be made easier with a series of specific steps. If I start with that key idea, I'll avoid much useless wheel spinning and research of material I'll never use.

The next step is to organize the parts of the thesis sentence. Time-management expert Alec Mackenzie states that the more time one spends in planning and organizing a task, the less time it takes to execute it. This holds true for writing. Many an educator has tried to dash off a report, memo or letter without a clear plan. This is a little like setting off on a trip without a map. Short trips to the grocery store are no problem, but driving to a distant and unknown campground can be more difficult than it first seemed.

ORGANIZE TO SAVE TIME

If you're writing a note to a colleague, you probably don't need an outline. But for most writing, an outline is a great help. The outline was something most students endured in grade school because the teacher demanded it. Students often wrote the paper first and then organized the outline. That was not what the teacher had in mind.

Many students dropped the outline as soon as they could because it seemed like such a hassle. Even the best writers abandoned the outline for years and then revived it to better organize their writing. Pulitzer prize winner Jon Franklin says: "I developed a phobia about outlines, and my ability to cope with them; as a result I wasted at least five years of my writing career proceeding on the assumption that outlining could be avoided." Franklin drives home the point that outlining makes writing much easier: "An outline, you see, has nothing to do with Roman Numerals. It is simply a scheme, or a set of procedures, that you use to sort out your thoughts and analyze your story before you sit down to write.

Writers who don't outline often become victims of what Franklin calls "spaghettiing." The nonorganized writer is fine for a while but soon finds that ideas start falling back on each other, much like a plate of spaghetti. The disorganized paper has no clear-cut beginning, body and conclusion. Thoughts that seemed so lucid at first start getting jumbled. The outline doesn't have to be long and complicated. It's a roadmap that gives a clear sense of where a writer is going. The outline may change in the course of the journey, but that's fine because the outline is designed to be flexible.

Start by composing a one-page outline with everything you know already about a topic. Do this before you do any necessary research. Put your thesis sentence about a fourth of the way down the page or the screen of the word processor. Then below the thesis sentence, write in the two or three main points you'll use to develop the thesis sentence. Leave room at the top for your lead and leave space between the main points. If a good introduction comes to mind, write it down. If it doesn't, don't worry about it, because you'll find it later during your search for material.

Match the outline format to the kind of piece you're writing. This chapter fits a topical format so that's what I used. Below is how the first outline looked: Thesis sentence: Writing is hard, but it can be made easier with a specific series of steps.

I. Outlining key ideas

II. Researching

III. Writing the first draft

IV. Revising and polishing into a final draft

In his Pulitzer Prize-winning story "Mrs. Kelly's Monster," Franklin uses what he calls a complication/development/resolution format. Franklin tells how surgeon Thomas Ducker gambled by operating on a tangled mass of abnormal blood vessels in the brain of 57-year-old Edna Kelly. Franklin takes the narrative from the minute Dr. Ducker gets up until the complicated operation is finished (*Writing for Story*, 28). Franklin's outline looks like this:

Complication: Ducker gambles by operating on the "monster."

Development:

1. Ducker enters brain

2. Ducker clips aneurysm

3. Monster ambushes Ducker

Resolution: Ducker accepts defeat.

How to Take the Pain out of Writing for Teachers and Students

If you write a one-page outline before doing any research, you'll save time because you don't have to look up material you'll never use.

Writer's Block

Sometimes the organized outline doesn't work because of writer's block. No matter how hard you've tried to get something organized, nothing comes. The muse of inspiration is sleeping on your shoulder.

If that happens, wake up the muse with the branching or spoke system. Draw a "flat" circle in the middle of the page and write the thesis sentence inside. Then draw lines that stretch to the circle. Put down a single idea on any one of the lines. Don't be concerned about order at this stage: let the thoughts tumble out.

Let's say you've been asked to write a paper for a professional conference and you have a three-week deadline. The topic is sexual harassment in education. You've decided that the key idea you want to convey is "Sexual harassment is a serious problem in education and there are some practical ways to help prevent it."

After this brainstorming, sit back and see what you have. Notice how the ideas logically bolster the thesis sentence in the circle. Then line up the points in outline form.

Research the Easy Way

Armed with the one-page outline, you're ready to find material you can use need and develop your thoughts almost any time. Let's say you have to write a report for parents explaining and promoting the new "mini-course" program at your school. Your principal tells you that students will be given the chance, during the spring term, to take short courses ranging from mountain climbing to cooking. You have a week to get the report in.

So how do you get going? Sit down and compose a one page outline based on what you already know about the program—and what you know may not be much. You've heard about the program in other schools and the principal gives you a list of the twenty proposed mini-courses.

Your one page outline might look like this:

> Thesis sentence: Our school is beginning a series of short courses that we believe will be of great benefit to your children.

I. Brief background of successful mini-courses at other schools
II. Our program
III. Benefits to your child

Writing the First Draft

For the first draft, work to be clear, concise and conversational. Write like you talk. Don't worry about perfection the first time through. You can fine-tune later during revision.

I find it helps to imagine that I'm explaining something to a good friend or student. If I'm clear and don't waste words, the first draft usually goes quickly and well—even though I know it will need polish later.

WRITING; TOOLS FOR THE FIRST DRAFT

You can use at least three tools to write: pen/pencil, word processor, or Dictaphone. All will do the job, but some are far faster and less tiring than others. Consider the following facts. Most people write longhand at about 35 words per minute. Good typists cruise along at about 65 words a minute. A word processor will get the speed up to 75 and most can talk coherently at around 125 words per minute. But humans think at 400 words a minute. The closer the writing speed is to thought speed, the faster and clearer the writing. E. B. White says: "Writing is, for most, laborious and slow. The mind travels faster than the pen; consequently, writing becomes a question of learning to make occasional wing shots, bringing down the bird of thought as it flashes by" (Strunk and White, *Elements of Style*, 69).

If you have the luxury of someone else to type your material, you can save time by dictating the first draft, having someone transfer the tape to the word processor and then editing yourself on the computer. Compose the first draft rather quickly and let your right brain do the work. Henriette Klauser says in her book *Writing on Both Sides of the Brain*, "Remember, the key to writing fluently is to separate writing from editing. Rapid writing—letting the words spill out without stopping to critique or correct or rearrange—is one dependable way to keep the two functions apart."

Editing and writing at the same time is a habit many find almost impossible to break. If you stop either to admire or chastise your work, your thoughts can get jammed because you're asking both sides of the brain to work at once and they're not good workmates. Let the free and easy right brain pour out the ideas with the sure knowledge that the more stern left brain will come in later to do the important work of polishing and editing.

After you've finished a first rough draft, let the work simmer—preferably overnight. If you can't afford that long a stretch, give yourself some time away from the draft so you see it from a fresh perspective.

Experts on writing emphasize that good writing is rewriting. Most readers don't realize that most published works have been polished and refined at least three times. Ernest Hemingway revised the last page of *A Farewell to Arms* thirty-nine times until, as he put it, he "got the words right."

The first time you read the rough draft, look only for those obvious errors that would embarrass you if anyone else read the paper.

The second time through, trim the less glaring but still obvious mistakes. These could include a vague phrase, a grammatical error or repetition of the same word three times in the same paragraph

On the final edit, get all the words right so that your writing is smooth and clear. At this stage, prune all the words you don't need. If you have to stop to understand what you wrote, the words need fixing. Or if a sentence or paragraph is clear but dull, spice it up with an intriguing example. Theodore Cheney emphasizes that the revision stage can be one of the most enjoyable parts of writing. You have the main ideas on paper—or word processor—and then you can polish what you've done. He reiterates that most professionals "write in haste, and revise in leisure." Cheney shows how any writer can polish her prose by cutting clutter, rearranging ideas, and finding more accurate words to convey ideas. On a first draft, a writer almost always uses more words than she needs. Cheney says, "Seventy-five percent of all revision is eliminating words already written; the remaining twenty-five percent is improving the words that remain" (*Get the Words Right*, 1).

Some words lend themselves more readily to the knife than others. Adjectives often don't do much for a noun. For example, an administrator doesn't have to state "My personal secretary will contact you" or "Our basketball coach had a tall mountain to climb." Mountains are always tall. If you need to stress that the mountain is steep, go ahead and add the adjective—not all mountains are steep.

Letting an essay simmer can uncover some organizational problems that were not evident during the first draft. Paragraph one might be better as paragraph three. At this stage, it might help to look again at your outline to see if you covered what you wanted in an order that is clear to the reader.

A word processor is a blessing during revisions. With a push of one or two buttons, you can move paragraphs around with ease. No more cutting and pasting. No more retyping the whole manuscript from the first rough draft.

During a final check, ask yourself if the words you're using are the most accurate to get your meaning across. If you've picked the word that most accurately describes what you want to say, leave it. If the word is vague and abstract, find a word that is clearer and more concise for the audience. For example, when writing a memo to faculty I might ask for a *succinct* response. For fifth-graders, I'll get blank stares so I ask for a *short* response. "Succinct" is a more precise word but most grade-schoolers won't understand it.

As a rule, short words are easier to read than longer ones—even though educational writing is riddled with the official style that favors big words. Use small words where you can; if a long word says just what you want to say, use it. Short words, however, will give you your best mileage.

Special Problems: Contractions and Personal Pronouns

Most writing experts maintain that contractions are fine if your writing is informal. If you're writing a paper for a graduate school professor who is allergic to contractions, you don't have much choice. If you're not boxed in by an authority figure who hates contractions, you still have to make a choice about using them. If you're not quite sure whether to write "let's say" or "let us say," read the words out loud and listen to how they sound. Then choose the form that sounds the best. If the formal version sounds stiff, use the contraction. But if a contracted form like "I'd" sounds too casual, stretch it out to the two word version "I would" as in "I would prefer we meet right after class."

Some writers believe that if they use contractions, they should do so all the way through the piece. Again, let the sound be your guide. One sentence might read "you've come a long way" and the next "you have what it takes to excel." To write "you have come a long way" sounds slightly rigid. "You've got what it takes" is too breezy. It's all right to mix contractions with formal use.

Personal Pronouns

Until recently, writers were forbidden, under the penalty of a bad grade or a scowl, to use the words *I* or *me*. The preferred way was "the author." But if good writing is clear, concise and conversational, "the author" sounds awkward. Personal pronouns are now widely accepted in the best places. If you're taking a course from a taskmaster who still insists on "the writer" or "the author," bite your tongue and use it. Better to conform than to get a bad grade for an idea that is not worth the fight.

Checklist for revision

Below is a checklist of those items that help guarantee good writing:

1. Is the lead strong? Do I grab my reader's attention in the opening sentence?
2. Is the writing clear? Would a reader have to work to understand what I'm trying to say?
3. Am I using more words than I need? Good writing relies primarily on nouns and verbs rather than adjectives and adverbs.
4. Am I using, for the most part, the active instead of the passive voice? The passive voice is usually flat and hides who did what to whom.
5. Given a choice of two words that mean the same thing, do I pick the shorter one over the longer?
6. When I read the piece out loud, does it sing—or at least flow? Does it have a nice conversational rhythm?
7. Are the grammar, spelling and punctuation correct?

One Last Look

If you've organized, researched, written a first draft and polished what you have, your paper should be in good shape. Read it once more to catch any typos or spelling mistakes that may have slipped through undetected. One way to spot them is to read the piece backwards, word for word. When we read left to right, we absorb thoughts in chunks so it's easy to miss a typo or spelling error.

If you can, get someone else to read the piece. Almost always, another person will catch something you missed. Small errors have an uncanny way of hiding themselves on a first or second reading, and someone else can find them when you can't.

READ THE BEST WRITING

Another way to make writing a pleasure and not a pain is to read or re-read the best books on the subject. The classic manual on good writing is Strunk and White's *The Elements of Style*. This gem is a summary of the rules E. B. White learned from his English professor William Strunk. Over two million copies of the book have been sold and it remains a treasury of rules and a model of clear writing.

On a par with *Elements of Style* is William Zinsser's *On Writing Well*. Zinsser taught writing at Yale, and has been an editor and author of thirteen books. He's a superb model of what he teaches. His writing is clear, concise, practical, and entertaining.

In addition to reading books about writing, I find it most helpful to immerse myself in good writers who excel in descriptive nonfiction. Some of my favorites are Annie Dillard, Joan Didion, Jon Franklin, and Paul Theroux.

HELPING STUDENTS TO WRITE

Many students fear writing almost as much as they dread public speaking. Such fear is understandable because for years, many teachers taught writing as a process that must follow thought. They told students that if they wanted to get their ideas on paper, they needed to plant them in their mind first. Most of us learned that fuzzy thinking produces fuzzy writing—and that's correct. Ideally, we would think a brilliant thought, organize it and then write it down. But most people don't have a clear and complete grasp of their ideas—especially at first. A college student may have a hazy notion of why he believes his school should give up its investments in South Africa, but he isn't quite sure of how to express his ideas in a letter to the editor. Writing can help him crystallize his thoughts, especially if he starts to organize what he knows.

Just as teaching a subject is sometimes the best way to learn it well, writing becomes a way of refining thoughts. Experts like William Zinsser

How to Take the Pain out of Writing for Teachers and Students

and Lucy McCormick Calkins have shown that writing to clarify ideas improves both thinking and writing.

Educators can pass on their own writing skills to students. At almost any level, teachers can encourage their students to write and not fear instant correction. They can go on to help students organize, research, write a rough draft and edit. Instructors have to adapt to the grade level, but every grade provides the chance for improving students' writing skills.

More and more educators are promoting writing at an earlier age. Kindergarteners now dictate stories about their favorite animals. Sue Rainer teaches first and second graders. She says: "It's important for children to learn that writing is just like talking, that it's really speaking on paper" (Wilbert, "The Right Way"). Third graders spin out essays about the moon or their trip to a museum. Youngsters are writing first and mastering grammar later. This technique has produced two results: students are less afraid of writing and they're writing better because they start earlier.

For young children, the organization stage can be thinking about ideas they want to put down. If they have an experience they want to write about (a birthday party or a trip to the ranch), they can think about what they want to say and then put the words on paper. As they grow older, children can learn some of the finer points of organizing—the need for a thesis sentence, the proper order of an essay and the function of an introduction, body and conclusion. Teachers can help them write without tension. Instead of correcting every mistake, instructors can let students express their ideas first and later show them how to eliminate errors of spelling, grammar and syntax.

Many schools have introduced "writing-across-the-curriculum" programs in which instructors from diverse disciplines teach their students to write better. Science instructors insist on clear explanations of the material they teach and history profs require lucid prose in student papers.

Without the pressure to always be "correct," students appreciate and enjoy writing. After attending a writing "rally," one second-grader said, "I really like to write. When you write, you get to do what you want, you get to use your imagination." Instead of feeling straitjacketed by rules, children have an outlet for their highly creative ideas.

Both teachers and students can make their writing easier, faster and better. If joy in teaching comes from passing on the good news, showing students how to write better is a gift students can utilize for the rest of their lives.

7

Organizing, Planning, and Time Management for the Teacher without Much Time

> "Take care of the minutes and the hours will take care of themselves."
>
> —Lord Chesterfield

ONE TEACHER DESCRIBED IT as the hardest part of her job: "Tell me how I'm supposed to get everything done. I have to prepare classes, teach five hours a day, correct papers, patrol the lunchroom, go to meetings and try to have some kind of home life." Managing time is hard for any busy professional but it can be especially trying for teachers who have to fit so much into a day and still have some energy left.

Experts have suggested numerous ways to save time. Used daily, these methods increase productivity and reduce stress—two major benefits for the busy teacher.

PLANNING

Educators have been told to plan their lessons, their days, weeks, and academic year—so planning is nothing new. But the trick is to apply the best techniques to those areas that will really save time. Some teachers know how to organize a lesson plan, but find it hard to coordinate a whole academic year. Others are good at the big picture, but struggle with a lecture or faculty meeting.

One teacher put it very well when she said: "I find freedom in structure. If you have a plan, you can always deviate from it if you want. But you can always go back to the plan if you need to." Planning for a teacher is like a good insurance policy. We don't think about it most of the time, but it's there when we need it.

Organizing, Planning, and Time Management

Planning Time Chunks

If you can get a grip on chunks of time, the battle is more than half won. The teacher who plans the year, semester, month, week, and day has control. And control tames stress. Less stress means more productivity. More productivity means greater satisfaction on the job.

In the 1920s, Charles Schwab, the president of Bethlehem Steel, invited a consultant named Ivy Lee to his office. He asked Lee to show him a way to get more things done in the time available and told him "I'll pay you any fee within reason." Lee gave Schwab a piece of paper and told him to write down all the tasks he had to do the next day and number them in order of importance. He said, "When you arrive in the morning, begin at once on No. 1 and stay on it till it's completed. Recheck your priorities; then begin with No. 2. Make this a habit every working day." Lee suggested that Schwab should have his staff follow the same procedure. "Try this as long as you like. Then send me your check for what you think it's worth" (Mackenzie, *Time Trap*, 39).

After a few weeks of using the system, Schwab mailed Lee a check for $25,000, with his thanks for giving him an idea that was one of the most useful he had ever heard. When some of Schwab's friends said they were surprised that the president would pay such a high fee for such a simple idea, Schwab responded by saying that the simple idea had been the most profitable of the year. Such a plan helped Bethlehem Steel earn over $100 million in profits.

Educators aren't presidents of steel companies, but the priority system works just as well for them. A teacher's day is filled with activities and interruptions. Drop-in visitors, telephone calls, and unanticipated crises compete with course preparation and classroom performance.

Alan Lakein has refined the priority system of Ivy Lee into what he calls the "A, B, C" method. Lakein suggests that the busy professional start by setting specific goals for the day, week, and month. The more specific the goal, the better chance of choosing those activities that will reach the goal. If a college teacher wants to write an article every three months, she decides how much time each day she needs to devote to her writing. She then sets up a schedule based on that time and sticks to it. Let's say she knows, from past experience, that it takes about sixty hours to plan, research, write, and polish an article for publication. Therefore, she has to log five hours each week for three months to reach her goal. She may write an hour every day or two and a half hours twice a week. She also makes her writing a priority and insists that nothing interferes with it. If she stays with it, she'll finish on schedule.

To apply Lakein's method to your own circumstances, begin by writing down specific goals and then a "to do" list. The goal might be to organize an all-day fieldtrip for a political-science class. The "to-do" items could include arranging transportation, making appointments with the mayor's office, taking care of the lunch, preparing handouts, and the like. The next step is to prioritize the items A, B, C. Put an A behind those tasks considered most important. Less important but non top-priority projects get tagged with a B. If a task doesn't fit in the top two categories, give it a C. You can also write subcategories like A1, A2, etc. to mark them in order of importance.

Lakein also recommends that busy professionals have a "C" drawer, out of sight for items like brochures that can be read on a lunch break. Such items tend to clutter a desk and distract from priority projects. Many find it useful to mark down only A or B jobs and to automatically drop a C item in the drawer for later attention.

Once the "A, B, C" system becomes a habit, you should be able to ask yourself at any given moment: "Am I doing right now what I decided is most important?" You may be having a coffee break in the faculty lounge, but you planned that into the schedule. But if you're taking a coffee break at a time when you planned to work on an "A" project, you would want to go back to your top priority.

You don't have to be a slave to the priority system. It's a tool to keep on track and no one but you is checking to see if you follow it. The system's main benefit is the control it provides. It assures the user that whatever task she's doing at the moment is the one she should be doing. Such assurance allows her to focus on that task without worrying about the others.

Making Minutes Count

Some people believe they have to have large blocks of time to get tasks finished. According to Lakein, professionals often put off the "overwhelming A" because they think they need a long, uninterrupted span. If they have a ten-page departmental review due in two weeks, they try to arrange some two-hour blocks. Ideally such blocks are a big help. But most teachers know that they rarely get all the time they need. A variety of interruptions intrude—an unexpected meeting, a sudden conference with parents, the three-day flu, etc. If you find the hours gobbled up by the unexpected, don't despair—take advantage of the minutes.

Lakein discusses the "overwhelming A"—the huge project—and then suggests a way to handle it when you know you don't have long stretches of time. Called the "Swiss cheese" method, Lakein recommends poking holes in the task. Let's say you have a week to prepare an eight-page memo justifying all the departmental money requests for the next year. But given your schedule, you can see only one or two large chunks of time available between now and the day the report is due in the principal's office. Grab whatever time you can. If you have only fifteen minutes before the next commitment, use that time to outline how you want to frame the report. Or gather last year's budget figures to see what you spent and what you'll need for the next year.

WORK SPACE AND TAMING PAPERWORK

If setting priorities saves time, so does a well-organized work space. Despite what one poster proclaims, neat desks are not signs of sick minds. A teacher's desk can resemble a bomb site or a Swiss bank—or somewhere in between. A few educators find that clutter makes them feel homey—because their desks look like their homes. But clutter can waste time because it takes so long to find items in the mountain of mess. Experts caution against becoming a "time nut" or an ultra-neatnic, but an efficient work space will save many hours over a school year.

A desk strewn with thirty-five or more different pages is a certified time-waster. Over a period of months, clutter can cut deeply into a teacher's schedule and managing untamed mounds of paper can test the sanity of the most dedicated professional. A misplaced file or lost memo from the principal wastes time and creates stress.

One barometer for measuring efficiency with paper is to count the number of times you touch a piece of paper. Over a three-day period, the average professional can pick up a letter twenty-five times. The ritual includes the first time he put it on his desk, the six or seven times he shuffled it with other papers, and the times he tried to find it but couldn't. All those moments add up. Combine that with the fifteen minutes of sheer stress incurred during the period it was lost, and it's easy to understand how one letter can create such havoc.

One practical way to organize paperwork is to place a three-layer rack on one side of the desk near the edge. Reserve the top rack for "A" projects—those considered most important. Keep the middle for correspondence—any letter, memo or note that has to be answered. The bottom level holds "B" items. Placing the correspondence rack just below the "A" rack serves two purposes: it visually separates "A" from "B" projects. It also provides a convenient place to store correspondence you need to answer. Instead of taking up space on the desk, a memo or letter can be tossed into the middle rack and then retrieved when you want it. As a bonus, the memo doesn't take up distracting space on top of the desk.

When a piece of paper arrives, you can dispatch any item by putting it in the "A" rack, the correspondence slot, the "B" rack, or the "C" drawer. Then you can quickly retrieve when it's time to do something with it.

Most desks have other objects on them like a stapler, paperweight, or desk calendar, but the center can be reserved for the project that needs immediate attention. The center provides visual confirmation that a project is the most important at the moment.

Filing

There are many sophisticated ways to file tests, papers, and correspondence, but two of the most useful are the traditional filing cabinet and a computer disk bin. Items like class handouts, student academic records, and correspondence can be stored in a standard four-drawer filing cabinet with each drawer organized according to a general category. For example, the top drawer contains general files arranged in alphabetical order. The second houses documents for each student advisee plus information dealing with an academic field. The third drawer is divided into two sections. The front half has papers that can't be stored on computer disks. The back half holds information on outside professional work. The bottom drawer contains class handouts arranged in alphabetical order. A teacher can organize materials any way she wants, but the key is to store them so she can find them quickly.

If possible, store material on a computer disk. Anything you can put on a disk will save space. Each disk has a catalog showing exactly what it contains. All you have to do is slip the disk into the computer and bring up the catalog by pushing a button. When you find the pathname of the project (i.e., final exam), retrieve it and see what you have. If you want to make changes, you can do so quickly.

Delegating

One of the best ways to save time is to give work to someone else who can do it just as well or better than you can. When I began as a director of summer school at Gonzaga University I enjoyed assembling the summer catalog. I chose and arranged the photographs. I wrote some of the copy. My expertise and experience consisted of a year as sports editor of my high school newspaper.

Setting up the catalog consumed time from other important duties. Working in the office was a college sophomore who had a much better sense of how summer catalogs should look. With some reluctance, I turned over the editing and layout. She did a better job with the task.

Delegating succeeds only if you can find qualified people to do the needed work. A teacher can spend hours trying to undo the damage done by an incompetent helper. On the other hand, much talent goes untapped because teachers are reluctant to give up certain assignments to others equally or better qualified. Besides secretaries and teachers aides, many highly qualified work study students can type, operate computers, correct objective exams, answer the phone, run errands and do a host of other jobs that will save a teacher countless hours over a school year. Taking time to train these aides is well worth the effort.

You might ask yourself: is there any job I'm doing now that someone else who can do just as well? Most educators can relinquish certain tasks and focus their energies on teaching. As an added benefit, delegated assignments often give people a sense of involvement and teamwork. Students gain valuable training.

Reverse Delegation

Mackenzie describes "reverse delegation." Sometimes called "delegation up," leaders in industry often take on and do jobs their subordinates should be doing. Instead of having employees make their own decisions, a manager's open-door policy encourages people to come and make the manager decide some issue. The same is true of teachers if they let others control them and their time. From family members at home to students at school, educators can take on more responsibilities than they should. Reverse delegation ties up their time, and makes others dependent on them.

A student says he can't figure out a math problem or is having trouble composing a coherent paragraph. Many dedicated teachers will solve the problem or fix the paragraph instead of giving some guidelines and then letting the students do the work. Students at school and children at home are skilled at getting adults to do what they should do themselves. It's fine to make sure the final product is right, but urging students to do the work is a benefit to them and a time-saver for the instructor.

BREAKS

Jim Brown was one of the greatest running backs in the National Football League. He also knew how to take breaks during a game. Brown would burst for ten or fifteen yards until two or three tacklers dragged him down. The great fullback would lie on the turf for a second or two before getting up. Then he walked back to the huddle like he was taking a Sunday stroll on the beach. When he ran with the ball, he hustled. But when he took a break, he rested and returned refreshed to the job at hand.

Breaks during the day can be time-savers because teachers return to work invigorated. Some instructors like to take a regular coffee break at the same time every day; others relax with two or three brief respites spaced throughout the day. These can include reading an intriguing article, talking to a friend or looking out the window at the clouds. How someone takes a break is not as important as taking one at the right time. Some kind of diversion can make a job a joy instead of a grind.

RELAXING AWAY FROM SCHOOL

Sander Orent is a physician who promotes holistic health. In his talks, he sells the advantages of play to prevent sickness and to keep the mind alert. He urges adults to play for one hour a day. Play can range from a bike ride to a game of tennis, but the player should do something she enjoys and not feel guilty about it. Someone might protest: "That's fine in theory, but I can't be a good teacher, parent, spouse, and community member and still manage an hour of play every day." Most professionals find play a time-saver because they can get more done when they're refreshed. The body will tolerate constant work only so long. At some point, it takes revenge in the form of extreme fatigue or sickness. All work and no play make Jack

Organizing, Planning, and Time Management

and Jill dull teachers because they're too tired. If you want to be more productive, take at least one day off a week. The Judaic-Christian custom of the Sabbath makes good sense. People like Lee Iacocca or top salesman Joe Gandolfo advocate hard work during the week but took at least one full day off on the weekend. They've concluded that hard-drivers need a respite so they can hit the deck running on Monday. Some teachers might object, "There is no way I can avoid correcting papers or projects on Sunday, even though I need a break." That may be true—at least on some weekends. But seven-day workweeks take their toll in burnout, frustration and poor teaching. In the long run, the seven day work week wastes more time than it saves.

MEETINGS

Parkinson's Law suggests that humans will fill the amount of time they're given to do a certain task, no matter how much time they have. Parkinson must have had meetings in mind when he formulated his law. Call an hour session to discuss a new kind of soap for the faculty restrooms, and participants will often spend the whole time on that topic. Take three subjects—new patrol uniforms, the annual faculty picnic, and a discussion of a policy on cheating—and participants will often take the same amount of time. Meetings are designed to solve problems, but they often create problems of their own. Teachers can't avoid meetings, but they can help make them more productive.

Two kinds of meetings can cut into a teacher's day—group and one-on-one. Administrators routinely call group meetings. Efficient use of meetings can benefit everyone who attends. But countless hours slip away because meetings are ill-planned and participants go off on numerous tangents as they plod through the agenda. The old adage: "A camel is a horse designed by a committee" underscores how meetings can be a bane rather than a boon.

At their best, meetings are a pooling of the clear thinking by all members to discuss important subjects or to solve problems. At their worst, they deteriorate into bull sessions or pseudo-therapy groups in which members air gripes or promote pet viewpoints.

So what makes group sessions more productive? Experts on time management advocate use of an announced agenda to let participants know what's coming. When teachers know topics three or four days in advance, a more productive meeting is usually guaranteed. If participants walk into a meeting room with a vague sense of what they're supposed to accomplish, the time is often wasted and members become frustrated. The average faculty meeting lasts an hour. The wise leader picks only those topics that can be covered realistically in an hour and saves other items for later.

The most important subject should be handled first because in an hour meeting, members will almost always spend over fifty percent of their time talking about the opening agenda item. If the first point is a discussion of whether to use white or colored chalk and the second subject is a discussion of faculty salaries, the chalk will get more airtime than the money. Paul Turner has written an article titled "Will Meeters Ever Prosper?" Turner begins by citing how many hours professionals waste because they don't plan meetings or conduct them well. Turner offers tips for running efficient meetings. They include:

1. Make sure the meeting is necessary and not just something we always do once a month.

2. Develop an agenda and send it out in advance of the meeting with directions on what each participant can do to make the session more fruitful.

3. Begin and end on time. If a topic comes up that is not germane to the agenda, the chairperson should acknowledge that the subject may be important but needs to be covered at a future meeting.

4. Near the end of each session, have some "action items" and designate specific individuals who are responsible for carrying them out.

5. Set up the time of the next meeting when everyone is present. This saves making phone calls.

ONE-ON-ONE MEETINGS

Teachers usually have little control over the time spent in faculty meetings because the principal, dean or chairperson decides when meetings will be held and how long they will take. But most have control over one-on-one meetings, like seeing a counselor about a student or meeting with the moderator of the Friday night student bus trip to the playoff game. How can you save time in one-on-one sessions? First, decide in advance

Organizing, Planning, and Time Management

how long you need to discuss a particular subject. If you really need to sit down with a colleague for two hours and hammer out a lecture for a team-taught class, devote two hours to the task. But minutes, hours, and days are squandered over the academic year with conversations that go nowhere. It's fine to relax with a friend and discuss the previous Sunday's football game if you need a break. But often business conversations turn into gab sessions. What started out as a discussion about discipline problems can drift off into gossip about what faculty member is on the verge of a divorce.

Time expert Alec Mackenzie advises stand-up meetings. Professor Gregarious walks into your office with the stated intention of talking about a necessary change in the college catalogue. But he usually starts with some business item—a prelude to his favorite pastime of complaining about the dean. If you stay in your chair and he sits down, a twenty-minute gripe session is guaranteed. If you stand up, walk around your desk and conduct business on your feet, the time gets cut by half. Stand-up meetings are efficient because they telegraph the message that this will be a business meeting and not a social chat. If you stay seated, you're trapped in your own workspace. It's considered tacky to announce after five minutes: "Okay, that's it—out of my office." Ironically, you have more control in someone else's workspace because you can end the session efficiently by looking at your watch, extending a warm farewell, and then leaving.

THE TELEPHONE

Alan Lakein has produced a twenty-nine-minute movie titled *The Time of Your Life*. In one of the opening segments, a hassled executive hears the phone ringing one more time, looks straight at the camera and then moans "If only I could do this." He then throws his phone in the wastebasket. Many teachers feel the same way. The phone haunts them at home and stalks them at work. It interrupts meetings, breaks concentration and can be a constant irritant, especially on busy days.

The telephone is a tyrant and a time-waster, but it can save time because educators can often handle business on the phone they otherwise would have to conduct in person. They don't have to travel to someone else's office, building, or city to talk.

Busy and productive pros have found ways to tame the telephone. If they're not in their office to answer the phone, they get someone else to take a message and then they return their calls in clusters. They begin each conversation in a friendly but firm tone which relays the message nonverbally: "I'm glad you called, but let's make this a business rather than a social call." Opening with a "Hi, how has life been treating you lately?" Or, "How 'bout those Dodgers?" often leads to five minutes of social chatter. Such talk is fine as long as both parties want that kind of dialogue, but the caller can save time by relaying the message that the purpose of the call is business.

Efficient people also plan the subject of their longer business phone conversations. They jot down the items they want to discuss. They often open with "Hi, Sarah. This is Steve Johnson and I have three items I would like to discuss with you if this is a convenient time." They then cover each topic with thoroughness and efficiency. If the conversation meanders down a tangent about the trivial, they pull it back to the subject.

SUMMARY

Experts in time-management advise "Work smarter, not harder." They also emphasize that hard work by itself does not guarantee results. An amateur mechanic can sweat, swear, and groan for two hours trying to replace a broken muffler and still not get the job done right. A pro can work at a comfortable pace for twenty minutes and fit the muffler perfectly because he knows what he's doing. He is also less stressed because of his skill.

Efficient professionals are more productive and relaxed. Most teachers have hectic schedules that allow little breathing time. Not all time-management methods work for everyone, but many of the techniques suggested by experts like Lakein and MacKenzie can help prevent burnout and make each day more productive.

8

Finding Joy Outside the Classroom

> "I would love teaching if only I could teach and not be bothered with everything that goes with it."
>
> —High-school instructor

MANY TEACHERS LIKE THE hands-on, face-to-face contact with students but endure the outside activities that go with the job. The list of nonteaching duties is long: faculty meetings, parent conferences, counseling sessions with students, coaching, glee club, drill team, committees, patrolling the halls, and selling raffle tickets. The type and number of activities depend on the grade level, but every full-time instructor is expected to take on added assignments. Primary school teachers might work on student Christmas pageants, raffle ticket sales, and magazine drives. Junior high teachers typically coach athletics, advise the yearbook or the school paper staff, and direct one of the school plays. High school instructors often advise various clubs, serve on faculty committees, help coach, and monitor lunch rooms. Community college instructors are expected to serve on committees, advise students, and get involved in community projects. Professors at four-year colleges and universities must combine classroom work with research and publication.

Teachers who enjoy their job see outside school activities as ways to interact with students and colleagues in different settings. Some of their happiest moments come during a talk in the cafeteria or a lengthy discussion on the bus returning from a football game. Outside activities go with the job. Attitude makes the difference between seeing extra duties as a grind or as a welcome diversion from teaching and another chance to have a positive impact on students.

Someone considering teaching as a career might find it useful to pick a grade level and then consider the whole package of duties. Assignments for a primary school teacher are different from a college professor. One person might relish contact with eight year olds, and someone else would find the experience a drain. Some love the "scholarly life." They like research, the musty smell of a venerable library, and the satisfaction of seeing their articles published. But others find research a bore and thrive on interaction with students. Teaching has many niches, and finding the one that yields greatest satisfaction leads to fulfillment. Few college students considering teaching as a career know the level they'll find most fulfilling. Imagining a number of settings and considering which one will be most satisfying helps to decide. Some educators have tried two or three levels until finally settling into the one that suits them best. I've taught on the high school, community college and university levels, and each one has had its own special challenges and joys. I ended up teaching at a small liberal arts university because I believe I fit there best. But it took a few years before making that discovery.

ACADEMIC COUNSELING

Most teachers are also expected to give academic advice. Many institutions emphasize academic counseling as a criterion for tenure and promotion. This service is especially important at the smaller colleges where individual attention to each student helps justify higher tuition.

Academic counseling takes special skill. Many high schools have full-time counselors who do nothing but help students plan their schedules and give advice about colleges and academic programs. But almost every instructor is expected to do some academic counseling.

Effective counselors help guide students through the rocky shoals of an academic curriculum. They offer advice about classes. They also help students who are struggling in courses and often teach them study skills. They help students plan for the future. On the junior high school level, a good counselor knows the requirements needed to get to high school. The high school counselor has a knowledge of various college programs and the advantages of going to one college over another.

Some students excel in huge universities, but others get swallowed in the large classes and a system that doesn't cater to the individual. Many high school seniors want to go to a mega-university without any practical knowledge of how the university works. They often ignore the challenge of five-hundred-student lecture classes and courses taught by teaching assistants who are also involved in their own graduate studies. High school seniors often know more about sororities, fraternities and football games than what it takes to earn good grades in a university. Many an eager freshman has gone off to the large university in September and has come home at Thanksgiving overwhelmed by an inability to balance studies with the many other activities competing for attention.

A wise counselor knows this scenario and may gently steer a student to a community college or a four-year college that will better serve individual needs. A community college may lack the greater prestige of a large, well known university, but the two-year school is one of the best values in higher education. Instructors are well trained, highly skilled and dedicate themselves to teaching over research. Students can get a superb education at a community college and then transfer to a university.

PERSONAL COUNSELING

Teachers who are outgoing and friendly will have students come to them with personal problems. Counseling can get sticky if an instructor becomes too involved in a student's personal problems and attempts to play the role of professional counselor.

Marilyn Underwood, a former teacher who became a full-time highschool counselor after earning her master's in guidance and counseling, conducts a workshop called "Effective Counseling for Teachers." Marilyn remembers she did a great deal of academic and some personal counseling as a teacher because students often came to her with problems. Very outgoing and caring deeply about her students, she recalls, "In those days, I didn't always handle counseling in the best way. I felt obligated to give students 'all the right answers' and to 'solve their problems.'" Often, she mentally carried her students' problems home with her and began to feel burned out.

After finishing her master's in guidance and counseling, Marilyn realized that classroom teachers frequently can't and shouldn't try to solve a student's personal problems. Marilyn advises teachers to listen actively when students present a personal problem and get them to consider their options. If the problem is severe, the teacher can refer the student to a professional who can work on a solution. Marilyn advises teachers: "We all need to know our own limits. If we can listen supportively and get students to consider their options, then we can be a real help. If the problem is more than we can handle, there are others available who have more background and experience. Let them take over. Sometimes, I've had to take a student by the hand and lead him to another professional who can do him the most good."

Paul Hastings, chair of a university Department of Counselor Education, agrees with Marilyn Underwood's advice. Paul teaches graduate-level counseling courses and has his own active practice. He doesn't counsel his own students about their personal problems. Instead, he refers them to another professional. He explains: "When a teacher tries to teach *and* counsel, he sets in motion a dual role and a wrong mix. An instructor's job is to dispense information, inspire learning, and make sure learning takes place. Teachers who try to solve a personal problem find they change roles with a student, and this shift makes it harder for them to evaluate objectively."

Paul emphasizes that if a student comes with a personal problem, the instructor can listen, offer support, and then refer him to someone who can help. Paul says, "As educators, we have often done a poor job of referral. If all I do is hand a student the phone number of the community health center, it may take the person two or three weeks to make an appointment—or the appointment never gets made. But if I make the phone call to someone I know or go with the student to the first session, I have provided some tangible help. That's why I have built up a network of counselors."

Teachers shouldn't try to act as therapists, but they can still help students with life planning decisions and advice on academics. High school and college students in particular can benefit greatly from the combined experience and wisdom of a teacher who has gone through the difficult process of finding the right college or career.

WORKING WITH PARENTS

Teachers and parents form one of the most important alliances in a s student's life.. Teachers in primary and secondary schools have more direct contact with the parents of students than do college professors. Most schools hold conferences where instructors and parents can work as a team to help students learn better. But even college teachers come in contact with parents through "Parent Weekends," informal discussion, and correspondence. College professors who get to know the parents of their students gain useful information and important insights.

Parents come in all varieties with different professional backgrounds and ways of dealing with their children. One sixth-grader may be the class hell-raiser, and his parents think he's a model child with a "teeny-weenie flaw or two." Other parents may have a bright, likable fourth-grader who is doing well in school, but who is not living up to their high standards. They criticize everything he does, and no matter how earnestly the teacher attempts to reassure them, they believe their child will be a failure and will disgrace them later in life. Both parents and teachers have insights and need to work together for the good of the children they love.

In today's culture, a teacher may deal with as many single parents as with couples. A majority of these single parents are women trying to juggle a job, raise their children, and maintain a personal life. This combination puts intense pressure on single parents to keep up with their child's academic progress and homework. Without intending to, single parents sometimes pass on anxiety to their children. Overwork and tension make it rough on children.

Many students show clear signs of stress like headaches, ulcers, stomachaches, and muscle tension. If they grow up in an atmosphere of shouting and short tempers, they'll be uptight when they get to school. Often families that seem so placid on the outside are teeming cauldrons of tension behind their carefully guarded facade. Children from such environments can have a hard time concentrating in school.

Kaye Aucutt is a special-education teacher who remembers the time a child told her the following story: "Mrs. Aucutt, I couldn't study for my spelling test last night 'cause Dad got drunk and everything at home was really terrible. First, I thought the cat was outside the house and I let my bird out of the cage. Well, the cat leaped out and killed my bird. My Dad got so mad he took the cat out in the garage and shot it. My Mom got so mad at my Dad that she shot the tires on my Dad's truck, so Dad took the car and left." Kay Aucutt arranged to let the child take the test at another time.

Becoming a parent is easy—people do it every second all over the world. But parenting well over a long period is hard, and few mothers and fathers get training in how to be good parents. They remember what their folks did and often model that behavior. Some might read Dr. Spock or other books on parenting and try to apply what they read. But most parents learn by experience and in the process, children can get bruised physically and psychologically.

Some parents care little about their child's academic progress while others hover over a child's every move. Both types can test the patience of the most dedicated teacher.

Neglectful parents can range from those who fail to feed their children to those who take care of physical needs but believe an education is something that has to be endured because the state requires it. Such parents rarely show interest in their children's academic progress and resent advice on how to become more involved.

At the other extreme is the oversolicitous parent who frets over everything the child does. Whatever the reason—insecure childhood, anxious-dependent personality, or the need for control—some parents want to be consumed in their children's activities. From folding their clothes the night before to packing their lunch to bundling them up on a cold day and walking them to the bus, these parents hover like a helicopter. Such people can be a challenge at a teacher's conference. If you suggest that seven-year-old Helen is good in math but weak in reading and writing, they immediately ask for information about a special Saturday course the child can take. Most skilled educators can reassure such parents that their child doesn't need a special course, but that reading to the child and checking her writing would be a big help.

A majority of parents see their children's education as a top priority and consider teachers working partners in this important job. Therefore, they usually listen to and respect what a teacher says about a child's work in school.

COMBINING OUTSIDE DUTIES WITH TEACHING

Variety helps make teaching a joy. A workday filled with classes, outside meetings, projects, and conferences flies by, especially if a teacher is immersed in each activity.

One secret to fulfillment is to savor each moment. Most people who remember "great days" recall that they were completely engaged in what they were doing all day long. They focused on the moment before them and each moment blended into the next. One hour they might have been painting; the next they were taking a walk and enjoying the scenery.

Finding Joy Outside the Classroom

Then they had lunch with a friend. Afterwards, they went back to their painting until they started fixing a gourmet meal.

A fulfilled teacher focuses on the task at hand. When she's in the classroom, she enjoys teaching. She then has lunch with colleagues. After classes are over, she coaches volleyball. Concentration on each activity makes the time fly and the job enjoyable.

BALANCING DURING THE FIRST YEAR

One of the best and hardest years of my teaching career was my first. I taught high-school English, Latin, and religion at a small school in Montana. I also had the boys' glee club, coached the freshman basketball team, and directed some student skits. I learned more about teaching in that first year than in the twenty-eight that followed. Physically exhausted but mentally charged, I thrived on the variety of duties. Such variety got me hooked on teaching. Never again would I do the same thing over and over.

Each hour at school was different and presented a new challenge: preparing a class, teaching it, talking to students, getting ready for a glee-club concert, or preparing the freshman team for a game. It didn't matter that our glee club had "delusions of mediocrity" or that the basketball team lost more than it won. Life was full and good.

During that first year, I remember feeling overwhelmed on occasion. For a first-year instructor on any level, the task seems enormous. You're given class assignments and then are asked if you would like to be moderator for the school yearbook, help out with the cross-country team, and be available for chaperoning Friday-night dances during the fall.

The first-year teacher is inclined to accept everything, because to do differently would telegraph the message that he's not totally dedicated to the school. Like certain college professors who give students more homework than they can handle, some principals overload new teachers. In such cases, the teacher may want to meet with the principal and emphasize that he wants to do a quality job in the classroom. Therefore he suggests that instead of having four outside responsibilities, he could take on two and do them well.

Most administrators respect teachers who lay their cards on the table this way. It is far better to be honest at the beginning about what one can do than to proclaim "Hey, bring on five classes, two coaching jobs, the school newspaper, and a faculty-committee assignment." Neophyte instructors who over-commit themselves often feel great stress and become convinced they can't do any one assignment well because their schedule is so heavy.

COMBINING TEACHING WITH ADMINISTRATION

Most administrators were teachers at one time. The majority of classroom instructors think about becoming an administrator for either a change of pace or a higher salary. Such choices can include full-time administrative work or a combination of teaching and administration. Deborah Kitching is one such person. She teaches fourth grade in Fort McMurray, a town of 34,000 nestled in northern Canada. Seventy percent of Deborah's time is spent in the classroom, and she is the vice principal the remaining thirty percent. She says, "My reason for splitting duties is a unique one. I love teaching, but I also like to have a positive impact on other teachers. As vice principal, I can interact with the newer ones by observing their methods and helping them get better. This presumes that I get along well with these teachers, but I work hard at establishing a strong bond with them. I find great satisfaction in passing along what I know about good teaching."

Department chairs are also often full-time faculty members, especially at smaller institutions. Many deans teach one class to keep their skills honed and to have a cathartic outlet for the rigors of administration.

After teaching high school for three years, community college for four, and university for five, I was asked to be director of summer school for one year while the university found a full-time person for the job. The one year turned into nine as I combined being a dean with part-time teaching. In retrospect, I'm glad I had the experience. It took me nine years as a dean and three as a department chairperson to realize that I was happiest with full-time teaching. I no longer begrudge administrators their higher salaries. For me, administration was a job: teaching has always been a joy.

9

Dealing with Problems as Challenges

Discipline, Grading, Plagiarism, and Difficult Colleagues

> "Be still, sad heart, and cease repining. Behind the clouds the sun is shining."
>
> —Henry Wadsworth Longfellow

SUCCESSFUL PEOPLE VIEW DIFFICULT situations in their lives as challenges rather than crises, and such a perspective helps explain why they enjoy what they do. Teachers who look on the tough parts of their profession with a positive attitude seem to be much happier than their disgruntled colleagues. Fulfilled educators confront the same problems as their unhappy fellow professionals, but they deal with them differently. They're able to accept and then transcend unpleasant circumstances.

Gene Neubauer was a school administrator in Oregon for seventeen years. He liked his work because he enjoyed people and saw problems as challenges to be overcome rather than as burdens to be avoided. Gene believed that solving problems was the heart of good administration. Some educators would like to eliminate the hassles that go with teaching—the discipline problems, conflict with difficult colleagues, school politics, criticism, and excessive work. But meeting and overcoming these problems produces a special kind of satisfaction.

Problems not only test an instructor's mettle, but make the job far more interesting. Teachers who look back on a long and happy career often agree that solving difficult problems was more fulfilling than having no problems at all.

Denny Yasuhara is one teacher who saw problems as challenges. He also convinced his students that hard work and high standards would make them happier in the long run.

Yasuhara had been a pharmacist until 1961, when he became a teacher. He found his twenty-eight years as a seventh-grade science instructor stimulating. Much of his satisfaction came from combining love with discipline. His students recall him as very demanding but he tempered high standards with an unusual concern for each youngster under his charge.

Yasuhara's students met to honor him for the influence he had on them. One former student, Bob Smith, said: "He taught us responsibility and accountability. He was more than a teacher—he was a mentor." Former student Cathy Nickle stated: "He's one of those teachers people remember for their whole lives. People are saying, 'He did the job my parents should have done, but he did it for 20 to 30 kids every year.'"

DISCIPLINE

Kidder describes the school year of Chris Zajac, a fifth-grade teacher in Holyoke, Massachusetts (*Among Schoolchildren*, 137). Chris Zajac often grew tired of being a disciplinarian, but "she never wearied of what discipline brought her. It allowed her to teach."

Some teachers have an easy time with discipline, and others find it the hardest part of their job. College professors rarely have to deal with disruptions. For the most part, students attend classes because they want to and almost never rebel. But discipline is different in primary, middle, and secondary schools.

I remember a year I taught undergraduate and graduate students and also offered a communication class at night for high-school seniors. During the course of a week, I interacted with high-school seniors, college undergraduates, and doctoral students. I discovered a paradox: the older and more mature the students, the easier the teaching. Doctoral students were a cinch because they were highly motivated adult professionals. If I prepared carefully, the class always went smoothly.

Such was not the case with the high-school students—a group of likeable but highly spirited seniors in their last few months before graduation. They had a severe case of "infectious senioritis," a malady that afflicts seniors two months before graduation. Symptoms of the disease include frequent bouts of apathy followed by bursts of enthusiasm. Attention spans are short, and restlessness breaks out after five minutes of class.

Dealing with Problems as Challenges

I taught high school for three years and have spent the rest of my time in the college classroom. As a result, I have long admired the dedication, patience, and pedagogical skills needed by junior high and secondary school teachers. Such instructors function on two levels. They have to get their subject matter across and also maintain discipline. Juggling both tasks well takes great skill.

Problems in discipline range from two students whispering in the back row to someone threatening a teacher with a knife. Incidents can include throwing spitballs, smarting off, making wise remarks that distract the entire class and sullen looks from students who want to let you know that they don't like you or your class.

What Makes an Effective Disciplinarian?

Physical strength and imposing size are rarely the ingredients needed for effective discipline. One very successful disciplinarian I knew was a woman five feet two and 105 pounds. One of the least effective was a six-five, 240-pound ex–football player.

The petite woman had a commanding voice, a firm manner, and complete control of the group. She didn't shout or badger but combined strong affection for her students with the clear message that she was in charge.

The ex–football player blustered a lot, but the junior-high students walked all over him because he wasn't consistent. One day he would try to be Darth Vader and then the next would soften to the point of letting students control the class.

Strong teachers temper their discipline with love and concern. The drill sergeant might maintain order, but students operate from fear. Children who know they're loved will tolerate sanctions far better than those who believe teachers don't like them.

Marsha Ripple taught fourth-graders in Portland, Oregon. She described her approach to discipline as positive.

> I begin by building strong self-esteem in the children. Every time they do something well, I praise what they did. Once I build that bond, discipline works well. I tell them what I expect of them and also describe what will happen if they break some important rules. Then I always follow through. If a child is acting up, I will start by walking to his desk and then talking to him individually. I apply the method that I believe works best for each student.

> One responds better if I tell him that I plan to call his parents if his behavior doesn't improve. For someone else, I might draw up a contract which spells out what the student is expected to do. Then we both sign the contract.

Good disciplinarians come in all sizes, shapes, and styles, but most share some common characteristics. They let their students know what is expected, and they're consistent. If they say they're going to apply a penalty, they do it. They don't begin class with a chip on their shoulder, but they're firm. During my month of cadet teaching in high school, my master teacher used to say, "Don't smile until after Christmas." While the advice might be impractical, the spirit is correct. Teachers who begin with an attitude of "Hey, if you're nice to me, I'll-be nice to you" attitude court disaster. It's easier to start with a firm set of guidelines clearly communicated to students and then to ease up once control is gained. If the instructor starts off as a softie, it's hard to get tough later on.

Confidence is one key to discipline. Confidence comes from preparation and the idea planted in the mind that the teacher is in charge of the class. Just as people are attracted to others who exude confidence, students feel assured when a teacher talks with the steady air of someone who knows who she is and what she is doing.

What if a teacher doesn't feel confident, especially at first? Act as though you're confident and little by little, the poise will become as natural as walking. Since most fear takes place in the mind and not in the real world, it helps to talk to oneself about being prepared and in control.

Some teachers use their voice to maintain order and others can do the job with a glance. One of the best disciplinarians I've ever known would stop in the middle of a sentence and rivet his eyes on an offending student. A hush fell over the classroom as the rest of the students turned around to look at the talker. Pausing for dramatic emphasis, the instructor would ask, "Are you through?" This strategy worked far better than another teacher's, who would periodically explode when students tried his patience. He would finally shout, "Sit down and shut up!" The tactic lasted about five minutes until another two or three students decided to badger him.

Mary Perizzo taught fourth graders. She says,

> I don't take discipline problems personally. We start off the school year discussing our 'bill of rights.' The students have rights and so

Dealing with Problems as Challenges

do I. Students have a right to learn and to feel good about themselves. The class and I talk about ways to insure those rights and then we decide on no more than four rules to help make sure those rights are being honored. Such rules might include raising a hand to speak, not demeaning other students and respecting each others' property. If we agree on rules at the beginning of the year, the rules are much easier to enforce.

Good teachers keep their students busy and make them accountable for what they do. Boredom is one of the most fertile breeding grounds for classroom problems. If students are kept occupied with activities that help them learn, they rarely cause problems. If they have to sit and listen to material delivered in a monotone, they get restless.

What Works and What Doesn't

Successful disciplinarians spend time carefully analyzing each class because they know students are not only different individually, but have their own personality as a group. Within the same semester, a teacher can have a class that sparkles and another that causes ulcers. Knowing this, the skilled teacher matches discipline to the students. She doesn't try to use the same approach with everyone. Just as a skilled salesperson carefully analyzes her audience to discover their needs and wants, so also does the good teacher. She observes and listens to find out what disciplinary approach works best.

Those who have trouble with discipline don't adapt to a particular group. They walk into a class of eager, well-behaved children with a chip on their shoulder and dare the class to knock it off. Or, at the other extreme, a teacher is faced with a group who are organizing a new street gang and concludes that these misunderstood kids need someone to be nice to them.

Not everyone clicks with everyone else, and this holds true for teaching. Most instructors can recount a horror story or two about a group of students who made life miserable. From the first minute until the end of the term, nothing jelled. Like a bad blind date in which the participants know from the beginning that the evening is going to be long, the ""bad class" experience is part of teaching. But a class is different from a blind date because the sufferers have to endure each other only for the evening they go out. With a class, teacher and students have each other for a long time.

Good teachers usually let students know from the beginning how much talking they'll tolerate. If they don't mind students whispering and passing notes while they're teaching, they don't have a problem. But if they find it irritating and disruptive because a few talk while they're lecturing, they let students know they want them to raise their hands first. Their approach is firm and businesslike.

THE DIFFICULT STUDENT

All instructors have had students who made teaching frustrating. Such students let teachers know they delight in making everyone as miserable as possible.

So why can the difficult student help make teaching a joy? Because the difficult student is often the one the teacher can most influence if she's patient, firm, and loving. Most rebels come from homes in turmoil and are leery of anyone giving love. Chris Zajac is a great teacher because she didn't give up on "Clarence," a fifth-grader she described as the most difficult student she ever had. Clarence hit other students, talked back to his teachers and often refused to do his schoolwork. Chris wasn't easy on him, but she kept working with him until he realized that someone really cared.

CHEATING

Some educators fight cheating on a daily basis, and others almost never encounter it. But of all the challenges that test an educator, cheating ranks near the top.

The causes of cheating vary. A few students will do anything to avoid failure. Some haven't studied and will copy from someone else or smuggle cheat-notes to class. Still others are honest most of the time, but the pressure to succeed is too great and they succumb to temptation.

Cheating comes in many varieties and students can be ingenious in finding new ways to beat the system. They scribble notes on their fingers and hide material in shoes, bras, belts, and buckles. Some glance at their neighbor's paper. Others try to copy from a textbook when the teacher isn't looking.

At times it's hard for a teacher to know if a student is cheating or is simply glancing toward someone else's paper without looking at it. Do you confront the student and take the risk that you're wrong because you don't have proof, or do you let it go? McKeachie says that when he's in doubt, he asks the student to move places without accusing him of cheating (McKeachie, *Teaching Tips*, 137).

Another approach is to call a student aside and discuss in private your suspicions about cheating. This approach is far less traumatic than exposing a student in front of the class, especially if the student vehemently denies the charge. Most humans will deny they've done something wrong, especially if their self-esteem is on the line.

GRADING

A junior-high-school teacher expressed what many teachers think: "Grading is always a misery. The need to categorize and pass judgment on kids rubs me the wrong way."

Grading, for many, has been one of the least satisfying but most essential parts of instruction. Solomon-like, teachers sit in judgment on their students' work. They write down *A*, *B*, *C*, *D*, and *F* on papers and final-grade sheets with the knowledge that such harmless looking letters can have a profound impact on a student's life. Grade-schoolers have to show their report cards to parents, who can make their life miserable if the grades aren't up to the parents' standards. High-school students worry that their grades will keep them from getting into the college of their choice. College students fret the same way because they know they have to earn a high GPA to get into medical, dental, or law school. Grades can make a big difference in landing a job because employers use a transcript as a plumb line to predict success.

Like many other aspects of teaching, grades can either help or hinder students. They can demoralize and instill fear. But grades can also be a tool in motivating students and in giving them an accurate idea of how they stand in class performance. Not all students are motivated to achieve high grades, but many are. Grades can be a barometer and a discussion point for teacher and student as they work together to try to improve performance.

If grading is hard for many educators, giving low grades is even harder. Sometimes students flunk classes, and the instructor has to verify that reality with an *F* grade. One teacher confessed to colleagues that he agonized over flunking one of his students because he knew the young man would be a dropout: "If I'd passed the kid, would he still be in school?

Why do we have to make decisions like that? It's so damn cruel. Why do I feel so bad?"

Most teachers know they've done the right thing if they carefully examine a student's work and then give the grade that most honestly reflects performance on a paper, test or an entire course. As much as educators want students to learn and succeed, they also know that a certain number will not. To give a student a passing grade when that mark would be dishonest is far worse than giving a grade that might make a student happy at the time. A professor at a large university explained that as bad as he feels when he gives an *F*, he knows that the student has flunked himself. Professionals fail in business and very few employers try to carry them on the payroll just to make them feel better.

Experienced teachers have found ways to reduce the stress that goes with grading. Suggestions include:

1. Tell students in advance what they need to do to get good grades. A speech teacher might say: An *A* speech will have the following elements—a clear thesis, strong organization, a good lead, a polished outline, about 80 percent eye contact, etc. A *B* speech will contain a clear thesis, good organization, a decent lead, eye contact over half the time, etc.

2. Let the class know you don't see grades as the most important part of the course but as indicators of how they're doing.

3. Keep the grading simple. Don't use an elaborate numerical grading system in an effort to be fair and accurate. Fit into the school's guidelines for grades, and make your best judgment about what mark to give.

4. Don't anguish over grades. Make a decision and sleep well afterwards.

FEEDBACK TO STUDENTS

Closely allied to grades are comments teachers make to students about classroom performance. Feedback is one key to successful teaching, but like grading, it has to be handled with tact and skill.

Wayne Booth is a college professor from the University of Chicago. One English teacher describes him: "Booth, 67, has a gray beard, a deep, calm voice, a national reputation as an authority on literary criticism

Dealing with Problems as Challenges

and the kindly manner of a Mr. Chips, the fictional teacher who inspired generations of English schoolboys " (Galloway, "Top Teachers Learn Lessons," A2).

Booth holds seminars for top English teachers in the Chicago area. Instructors, who at first feared handing in their work to such a distinguished literary critic, were surprised by his approach. One said: "The way he critiqued my papers has given me a model to follow. There are no red marks and comments in the margins. In effect, he writes a letter to you, beginning with what he likes about your paper. He is specific and clear." David O'Neill of Lane Tech High School said, "Wayne's erudition is buried—he is truly modest. He never once made a sarcastic remark. He is nourishing and gentle" (ibid.).

CORRECTING ASSIGNMENTS

During her first year of teaching, Lynda Kime said, "I'm definitely inspired. I love what I'm doing." But Lynda also confesses that the least favorite part of teaching is correcting papers: "It just takes so long. I don't want to sit and correct papers; I want to start working on something coming up that I'm really excited about" (ibid., 28). Many teachers see correcting papers as drone work: it has to be done, but it's not something that makes the adrenaline flow.

Correcting gets a little more bearable by knowing that feedback on assignments is one of the best ways to help students learn. If joy in teaching comes from making students better, correction combined with practical tips helps students develop their potential in any subject. If a fifth grader writes better, if a junior high school student knows how to solve math problems, or if a college sophomore understands accounting, such improvement often occurs because a teacher has taken the time to correct an assignment.

Facing a mountain of fifty papers the night before they're due to be handed back can depress the most dedicated teacher. Spreading corrections over a period of time makes the job easier. I find it helps relieve the strain to decide on a specific, reasonable date for returning the papers to students and then to divide the number of papers by the days until the promised return date. If I have forty papers to get back and give myself a week, I try to correct about eight papers per working day.

TEACHER EVALUATION

Students are not the only ones evaluated in school. In one way or another, instructors are graded, too. Administrators visit classrooms and make judgments about teaching performance. Students in most colleges routinely evaluate their instructors near the end of a course. Rank and Tenure committees scan teacher evaluations to help make judgments about teacher promotion and retention.

Evaluation can serve the same function for instructors as grading does for students because it measures teaching performance. Instead of avoiding evaluation, instructors see how they're doing. They may not agree completely with an administrator's or students' assessment, but they get some data that should help them improve.

The timing of evaluation is crucial. Most colleges have students evaluate instructors the last week of the course. Evaluation at the end of a term has a disadvantage because it's often too late to change teaching strategies for that term. Such feedback might be helpful for the next semester or quarter, but it doesn't provide specific information about how to adapt and improve teaching for the current class. One way to solve this problem is to ask students three weeks into a course to write down anonymously what they like about the course and what they would like to see changed. A teacher can start by telling students that she wants feedback from them.

This exercise can help in two ways. First, it sends out the message to students that an instructor values their opinion. And the teacher gets useful information at a time in the course when she can adapt and change if she thinks it is needed.

Another helpful way to improve teaching is to have a class videotaped and then to sit down and watch. Pretend you've never seen this person before and you walk into his classroom. What do you think? How clear is he, does he get his ideas across and keep the attention of the class? What do you like about the way he teaches? What would you change to make him better?

Don't be too hard on yourself by focusing immediately on what you see as flaws. Get the whole picture. Enjoy watching what you do well. Make notes of those areas that might need improvement—like more animated delivery, really listening to what students are saying, or keeping the class moving.

Dealing with Problems as Challenges

PLAGIARISM

One problem virtually all teachers face is plagiarism. Most students have a vague idea of what the term means, but often don't know exactly what plagiarism is or why it is such a serious breach of academic ethics.

In its simplest form, plagiarism is the stealing of another's ideas and presenting them as one's own. An obvious example would be of a fifth-grader who directly copies material word for word from the encyclopedia and submits it as his own report on Alaskan polar bears. But other, more subtle forms of plagiarism can creep into the classroom. A student knows that copying word for word is wrong, so he takes a passage and changes four or five words. Or a high school senior is in a rush to get a term paper finished, and does a close paraphrase of somebody else's work without acknowledging where he got the material.

WHAT CAN BE DONE?

Educators can't completely stamp out plagiarism, but they can reduce it. Explain to students in any class from grade school through a graduate program what plagiarism is and emphasize why it's such a serious problem. Faculty members have been fired because they plagiarized material for an article or book. Seniors in college have been denied graduation because they plagiarized a final paper.

A teacher can then go on and give some tips for avoiding plagiarism. If a writer uses someone else's exact words, she should put that section in quotation marks. If the same writer is not using the exact words of the author but is indebted for the idea, all she has to do is cite the work she used. This can be done in traditional MLA, APA, or Chicago formats.

An instructor can also explain what plagiarism is not, since some overanxious students worry about the problem and cite everything. It is not plagiarism to write down an idea familiar to almost everyone. Examples are that Aristotle was one of the great philosophers of all time, that Napoleon lost the Battle of Waterloo in 1815, or that a feeling of self-esteem is important for successful people.

Like so many other problems, plagiarism boils down to common sense. If the idea is your own, you don't have to cite it. If it is someone else's, give the other person credit.

THE DIFFICULT COLLEAGUE

Most people in education are pleasant, sincere, and easy to get along with, but occasionally a teacher will encounter a difficult colleague. Incompatibility is a problem in marriage, family life, and business. Teachers aren't exempt because they're members of a noble profession.

John Powell recalls a time when he walked with a friend to a newsstand to buy a paper. The man behind the counter tossed the paper to the friend and scowled as he did so. Powell's friend picked it up, smiled, and walked away. After this happened two days in a row, Powell asked his friend, "Why do you put up with the man's rudeness?" The friend responded, "I'm not going to let his behavior ruin my day. His rudeness is his problem, not mine" (Powell, *Why Am I Afraid to Tell You Who I Am?*).

Such a positive, detached response is hard during a conflict with a colleague, but it usually works best in reducing the conflict and in helping retain peace of mind.

Physician Redford Williams reveals that people who trust others and expect the best of them live much longer than those who treat others with hostility and suspicion. In his research, Williams found that hard-driven, type-A people are often worn down not so much by their intense activity but by anger and mistrust of others.

People who look for and expect the best in others not only diffuse hostility but feel more at peace with themselves. It's not easy to turn the other cheek, especially when a colleague is an antagonist rather than a supporter. But returning hostility for hostility not only prolongs a conflict but creates stress.

Not everyone on the planet likes us and approves of our ideas. You might be teaching with someone who lets you know early that friction will be the key factor in your professional relationship. Perhaps your personalities clash. Maybe the colleague doesn't think your academic standards are high enough. Perhaps you remind the fellow teacher of someone who beat him up in the sixth grade. People have numerous reasons why they don't get along.

One solution is to avoid the person, unless you have to come into contact with him every day. At times it's better to avoid someone who doesn't affirm you. Life is too short to be worn down by a fellow professional who demeans.

Dealing with Problems as Challenges

A second approach is to deal positively and kindly with the colleague when the two of you meet. If you get the familiar, cynical look that says, "I don't like you much," react by being calm and friendly. The civil approach may not solve the problem, but it won't spray kerosene on the flames.

A third approach is to ask the difficult person to meet at a time convenient for both of you. When you meet, explain your feelings about the relationship. You might start with a statement like, "I realize we have a problem, and I'd like to solve it. Here is how I feel. I would like to get your reactions also." This approach doesn't work with everyone, but often it does for two people who have been friends at one time but who have developed a problem somewhere along the way.

Sometimes it helps to try to understand the reasons behind someone's peevishness. Perhaps the person is having a hard day, and his mood has nothing to do with you. Or maybe the individual is the kind who fights with everyone, and you happen to be in his line of fire. Some people are obnoxious so they can have a reason to explain to themselves why no one likes them. If they were nice and nobody liked them, that realization would be too hard to bear. Their abrasive personality helps them justify why they have problems with others.

St. Paul's advice to the Corinthians applies well to difficult colleagues: "Love is patient, love is kind, and is not jealous. Love does not brag and is not arrogant, does not act unbecomingly; it does not seek its own, is not provoked, does not take into account a wrong suffered, does not rejoice in unrighteousness, but rejoices with the truth, bears all things, believes all things, hopes all things, endures all things. Love never fails" (1 Cor 13:4–7).

If you've tried every approach you can think of and nothing works, stay calm, be friendly, and don't let it wear you down. Someone else's ill will and feisty temperament shouldn't ruin your day, week, or school year.

10

Homework and Testing

> "A class, like a teacher, never stands still. It progresses, or it deteriorates. If it does not learn, it forgets."
>
> —Gilbert Highet

At the age of fifty-three, I decided to take up skiing. For years, I had wanted to learn but always had reasons for putting it off—too old, legs won't tolerate it, too expensive, etc. But I started taking lessons. Because I had to learn from scratch, the experience gave me some insights about how good teachers use testing and homework to reinforce material covered during "class-time."

I signed up for lessons at a place called Lou Lou's Magic Mountain in Spokane. Magic Mountain is a ski shop that features two long carpets designed to help skiers get the hang of the sport before they try the snow-covered slopes. The "six-pack special" featured six half-hour semiprivate lessons. I hadn't felt fear for a long time, but as I stood at the top of the rotating rug, I wanted to back out. Fear of falling and looking stupid dominated my brain. With some gentle urging from Karen, a nineteen-year-old instructor, I started wedging down the indoor hill. My legs soon got tired and I took a few falls, but I kept with it through the six lessons and went on to enjoy the sport in real snow.

Four instructors handled the lessons. All were good, but two stood out as exceptional teachers. Their instructions were explicit and clear. They praised me and my son Tony when we did something right, and they showed us how to correct our mistakes. Both emphasized the importance of reinforcement in grasping the fundamentals of this unfamiliar sport. They told us to visualize in between lessons the steps we had already learned. Then they tested us when we returned for the next round. It also helped to buy a videotape produced by Warren Miller, titled

How to Ski Better. As narrator, Miller encourages viewers to watch a specific technique many times until they've learned it well. The combination of lessons, visualization, watching the tape, and practice between sessions produced learning and the pleasure that comes from it.

Master teachers use homework and testing as tools to reinforce material and to measure whether learning has taken place in the classroom. Students can absorb data simply by sitting at their desks, but they learn better if they work between classes and are tested on a regular basis.

HOMEWORK

Professional trainers and classroom teachers know that reinforced material learned over a period of time sticks longer than a single workshop or class. Humans can hear a lecture on anything from French gourmet cooking to Bach's treatment of counterpoint and be able to tell friends about it right afterwards. But the forgetting curve starts dropping drastically within two hours after the lecture. Material that seemed so fresh and under control can vanish by the next morning. Homework helps keep material alive in the mind.

The term *homework* in many cases is a misnomer, because students often do their homework in study halls and never take a book home. Homework can vary from four minutes of "look over your spelling words for the next class" to three hours every night. I taught at Jesuit High School in Portland, Oregon, for two years, and teachers were expected to give students three hours of homework each day.

Outside assignments work best when they're linked directly to in-class material and serve to reinforce such material. A high-school English teacher might assign Charles Dickens's *David Copperfield* and then discuss the book in class. Between classes, he has students read selected chapters and might also ask them to write a brief paper on nineteenth century England to give them a flavor of how Dickens's characters lived. When he and his students have finished the book, he might schedule an essay exam to test both the content of the novel and the students' ability to write about their experience of Dickens. Sometimes called the "preview, study and follow-up method," this system has been used for years because it reinforces material covered during class.

Good teachers take pains to make sure homework is intriguing—or at least interesting—to students. Most students consider homework a drag, and a wise instructor is aware of the resistance to outside assignments. She tries to make her in-class presentation sparkle, and she's creative in making sure assignments sustain interest in the subject matter.

Math professor John Firkins had students write about their fear of math instead of limiting themselves to solving problems. Firkins taught college mathematics and had a reputation for helping students get over their phobia of math. In 1986 Firkins was named the Washington State Professor of the Year and also placed second in a national competition for teachers sponsored by the Carnegie Foundation for the Advancement of Teaching. I asked him how he used outside assignments for his courses. He began by telling me how much he likes teaching:

> I love what I do, and students tell me on course evaluations that if their teacher likes math so much, maybe there's something to it. I design homework to reinforce what I've covered in class. Instead of simply making students do a set of problems on their own, I give them a problem or two and then ask them to work in groups after class. I'm a great believer in cooperative learning because they have to work with other people once they start a profession. They can seek out information from anyone but me. My emphasis is on problem solving. I urge them to start by clearly describing the problem before they try to solve it. Then I ask them to write a paper outlining the steps they used to come to the solution. The papers don't always have to be about math. Sometimes I ask students to write about how their moods affect the way they tackle a math problem. I grade the paper on everything from clarity to grammar. Each student has to write a theme a week, and I'm pleased to say that thirty-five of my students have had their papers published.

In 1983 the North Carolina English Teachers' Association cited Richard Lebovitz as North Carolina's outstanding English teacher. (Macrorie, *Twenty Teachers*, 21). Lebovitz gets his students involved. Instead of having them write about the sea or a lighthouse, he has them write about their experiences with the sea and lighthouses. He's found that students write better when they look at topics from their perspective.

Marcia Umland used the same approach with first-graders. She doesn't concentrate on spelling and grammar as much as she encourages students to write about something relevant to them: "I try to teach practical writing. When something's wrong in the room, I get the kids to write about it. One girl says, 'I have to call my mom because she has my lunch money.' And I say, 'Write a note for the school secretary explaining the matter so she can call your mom, and we'll send it to the office with the roll call.'" Most students learn best and stay interested longer when they have to do something active. Getting students to read and study for tests is fine, but also having them build a model bridge or visit a police department stays longer in their minds. Science teachers have known for centuries that lab sessions reinforce material covered during lectures. More instructors in other disciplines have come to realize the benefits of hands-on learning.

In doing research for this book, I looked for common threads of good teaching. Almost without an exception, the best teachers were innovative in their homework assignments. Good teachers had their students dig deep and get personally involved. Stanyan Vukovich is a high school Social Studies instructor in Oakland, California. Many of his students are black. He said: "When I began teaching . . . I had high hopes that all my students would become scholars entering four-year institutions so that they could become leaders in the struggle for black liberation." But he soon realized that such a goal was unrealistic: "Some of my students didn't know where the Pacific Ocean was in relation to Oakland" (ibid.).

Vukovich found ways to get his students involved. In doing a segment on the pre–Civil War period, he divided his class into two newspaper staffs: one was the pro-slavery Charleston *Mercury* and the other the abolitionist *North Star*. He told each staff to do research and then write articles and ads typical of the pre-Civil War newspapers. He emphasized that he was not trying to defend a movement as indefensible as slavery but wanted his class to understand the issues in 1861. Students read primary sources in the library to get a better flavor of the period.

Vukovich met with both editors to assemble the newspapers and to make them as close as possible to the originals. Students learned how to write better and gained a profound understanding of slavery.

Only the most naive teachers expect that all students will read assigned books or articles. Teachers in the past few years have noticed a decline in students' desire and ability to read. Allan Bloom writes that "whatever the cause, our students have lost the practice and taste for reading. They have not learned how to read, nor do they have the expectation of delight or improvement from reading" (*The Closing of the American Mind*).

Students know they can play "reading roulette." They can skip a reading assignment with the odds in their favor that the teacher won't call on them in class.

They can't escape if they have to read and then produce something to turn in. A history instructor asks her students to read about Lee's surrender at Appomattox—an event which ended the Civil War. Then she asks them to write a one-page essay to prepare for a small group discussion. The title of the essay might be the following: "Did Lee Surrender Too Late, Too Soon, or Was His Timing Just Right?" Instructions might be, please give reasons for your point of view because you'll have to present your ideas in a small-group discussion.

Experienced teachers know that students don't always turn in homework. One of the least effective ways to handle this problem is to embarrass the culprits in front of the whole class. A better way is to outline clearly at the beginning of the term how outside assignments fit into the course and how they affect the final grade. Students often learn best through consequences. If they don't do their homework, their grade reflects the omission.

How Much Homework?

The amount of outside assignments depends on the class, the individual student and what other teachers in the same school are assigning. Homework can vary from almost nothing to more assignments than a student can really do in the time allotted. Some students are happy with almost no outside work and brag to their friends that they "never have homework." But they also have a hard time remembering material from class because there has been little reinforcement.

On the other hand, students can get so much homework that they can't complete it in the time given. This usually happens because teachers in the same school are not aware of what other teachers are assigning. The situation is more common in demanding prep schools and colleges, but can happen anywhere. If a student is taking five classes and each instructor assigns an average of an hour's homework, the student is overwhelmed. College students often find there are not' enough hours in the day to do every outside assignment. A teacher can help students avoid this pressure if he tries to find out what other teachers assign. Many instructors make

Homework and Testing

it a point to know how much overall homework their students are getting and then they adjust their assignments accordingly.

Passing On Time-Management Tips to Students

Some teachers help their students by showing them how to do homework efficiently. Joan Butler teaches fifth-graders and shows them organizational skills at the beginning of a course. She says:

> I find the homework goes much easier if I give each student a calendar of the coming month. Then I have them write down their homework assignments and the exams scheduled for that month. I also have them buy a pocket-size assignment book. If I give homework, the students immediately write the tasks in the book and on the calendar. The third item I have them get is a three-ring binder so they can separate each subject. Once they learn how to use all three, I find few problems with homework. Parents like the system because they can ask a child about homework and then see the assignment book.

Even first-graders can benefit from time management tips. Such tips can include, 1. Study when you're rested and not when you're tired. 2. Study in half hour segments rather than long stretches. 3. Establish a schedule and stick to it.

Parents and Students' Homework

Ginott recommends that parents should not become overly involved in their children's homework. He doesn't mean that a parent shouldn't respond to a child's request for help, but parents shouldn't hover and become preoccupied with outside assignments. Ginott suggests that homework should be primarily "between student and teacher." Parents can listen when students moan about homework. They can ask questions or provide emotional support when their children are frustrated with their inability to complete a problem or write a paper. But they shouldn't badger their children or do their homework for them.

TESTING

Few students will reveal how they're doing in class. An occasional brave soul might say, "I don't get this." But many students will feign understanding when they don't have the foggiest notion of what the teacher has just explained. Students are more likely to admit they don't understand material or to ask for more information if they know they'll be tested.

Objective, essay, and oral exams all have their strengths and weaknesses and teachers have to make choices about which kind will best fit their subject matter. Various tests have pluses and minuses in the time they take to write, distribute and correct. Objective tests are easy to correct but tedious to construct. Essay exams take less time to prepare, but require hours to read. Oral exams consume large blocks of time because they're usually given individually.

So-called objective exams have the advantage of being factual. If an instructor has covered the U.S. Constitution, she can test students on how much they know about the document. If a chemistry teacher has spent three classes discussing atomic energy, he can use the objective test to see how much information students absorbed from his lectures.

True/false, multiple choice and "fill-in" questions are more objective, but they also increase the student's odds of getting them right by guessing rather than by really knowing the material. True/false questions provide a better chance of answering correctly than multiple-choice questions. If the question is, "Napoleon lost the Battle of Waterloo in 1815. True or false?" the odds are 50% that the quiz-taker will get the right answer. If the question reads "Napoleon lost the Battle of Waterloo in: a. 1759; b. 1815; c. 1818; d. 1893; e. 1912" the odds are only 20 percent that a student will guess correctly.

No matter how hard teachers try to let students know what an exam will cover, they find land mines strewn in their path. An instructor presents a certain block of material—an explanation of photosynthesis. Students take notes and try to remember. She then gives the test and is surprised when students complain that the questions on the test did not match the material presented in class. In the "statements we'll never hear from students" category, is the following: "Mrs. Johnson, I want to compliment you on creating a test which covers everything you talked about in your lectures." Students often complain: "The material on the test is not what you talked about in class. Therefore your grading is unfair."

Essay exams allow students to show how much they know, since they're not limited to the material asked in the fifty or so questions on the objective test. The essay test also makes students organize and express in their own words what they have learned.

Homework and Testing

An essay test has its own set of problems. For starters, students can sometimes bluff their way through an answer without having really mastered the material. Over the centuries, students from all cultures have practiced the fine art of "slinging the bull." While most teachers can detect the "bluffer," a combination of weariness and 100 exams allows some students to slip through undetected.

Teachers must make a subjective judgment about the correctness of an essay answer. In an objective test, the score on an answer is always the same so it makes little difference whether the corrector is tired, rested, hassled or calm. But for an essay exam, a teacher might correct the same essay exam in the morning when he's alert and at night when he's tired, and the grades will likely be different.

The same essay answer would likely get five reactions from five different instructors. A student could write an analysis of Robert Frost's "The Road Not Taken" and hand the paper to all members of an English department. Rarely would the returned grade be the same from each instructor. Each of the teachers may be well qualified to grade the paper, but each also looks for different strengths and weaknesses.

The "halo effect" can also be a problem for some instructors. If a strong student has done well on the first two exams, a teacher might assume that number three will be just as good, even if it's not. Many teachers solve this problem by "blind correction"—making sure they correct and grade the paper before knowing who the author is.

Essay exams take a long time to correct. Many a bone-weary and soul-numbed teacher gets discouraged facing a desk-full of essay exams. Doing the job right takes concentration, alertness and a large chunk of time. Given the crush of deadlines and a plethora of activities, some teachers don't have the hours to devote to essay exams, especially if they've promised to get them back to students within a reasonable period.

The preceding may appear negative in a book written to underscore the joys of teaching. My purpose is not to discourage giving tests but to admit that after forty years of teaching, I haven't found the perfect exam and I'm more aware than ever that any kind of exam has some shortcomings. But I still value the exam as a useful teaching tool. I used to worry about the defects inherent in any exam. I don't anymore because I realize that no one drives the perfect car or owns a house without problems. But most people are willing to put up with the imperfections of houses and cars because they enjoy the many benefits they gain. Tests are like that.

They're not perfect, but they yield a number of advantages for students and teachers.

Testing as a Motivator

Lowman notes that "examining has a powerful effect on the way students study and the amount they learn during a course" (*Mastering the Techniques of Teaching*). Few students might study hard if they weren't tested, but most need the stimulus of an exam to stay on top of the material. If students know from the first day of class that they'll be periodically tested on material, even the most apathetic will pay more attention and may crack a book outside of class to avoid embarrassment on an exam. The best students anticipate meeting a challenge and being rewarded with a good grade. The majority may be tempted to slack off in their studies, but an impending test gets their attention.

Students usually focus on the material they know an instructor will give on the exam. A few live on the edge of danger and cram the night—or hour—before, but most are aware of a coming exam and will study accordingly. Lowman notes that many students have a need for challenges in their life: "Examinations, like athletic contests or artistic competition, satisfy these needs for many students" (ibid.).

An exam that produces a nice balance between mild stress and confidence born of preparation can be a good motivator. Students who anticipate an exam may feel some tension but the tension compels them to study.

Student Anxiety about Tests

Tests might be a strong motivator for most students but they can also create undue stress and fear in some. For this reason, good teachers usually explain why they're giving tests and demonstrate how students can study for them.

Students will take exams because they have to, but they'll take them more willingly if they know how a test fits into the course. Some teachers spend time explaining that tests are designed to both measure and motivate. Students are open to persuasion. If you offer them good reasons for doing something, they'll not only go along, but a few will do so eagerly.

Homework and Testing

Helping Students Take Exams

Effective teachers can go beyond merely giving and correcting an exam. They can review the material in advance of the test and pass on tips about how to study for it. Reinforcement is one of the keys to learning. An instructor presents material in class, reviews it before the exam, gives the test and then discusses the answers afterwards.

During the review, the teacher emphasizes what material she considers most important. Students listen better and can get a handle on what won't be covered in an exam. Students get frustrated if an instructor says little more than: "Make sure you know everything we've covered in the last month."

Instructors can show students how to take exams through note taking and listening. Some students have never been taught how to take good notes. They may have heard in the third grade that outlining is a good method, but then become overwhelmed when a teacher doesn't lecture from an outline. Some may take too few notes, and others may take too many.

Near the beginning of a course, a teacher can spend half a class period showing students how to take efficient notes. For example, she might tell them to match the note taking to the instructor. If she lectures from a well-organized outline, she tells students how to follow along. If she uses a looser format, she tells them to write short summary paragraphs.

An instructor might emphasize to students the benefits of keeping notes in a well-ordered three-ring binder. When exam time comes, they don't have to try to decipher their own jumble of notes or try to gather information from other students.

Tests and the "Fast Failure"

Tom Peters endorses "fast failures." He explains that in their drive for quality work, managers often insist that employees "do it right the first time." But often, the end product—microwave, automobile, or new vacuum cleaner—is a result of many "fast failures." The first ten or twelve attempts to get something right may fail, but each failure created an insight that helped produce the finished product. Without the freedom to fail, inventors would never finish their inventions. When asked how he could tolerate failing over a thousand times in his efforts to discover electricity, Thomas Edison replied: "I don't believe I've failed over a thousand times.

I've just found a thousand ways that electricity doesn't work." Edison worked until he got it right.

Teachers can apply the fast failure concept to the classroom. The fast failure allows students to see where they need work. If a teacher gives a test, corrects it and then hands it back with a *D* or an *F* and no comments, students know only that they've failed. But an instructor can use a poor exam to show students what they need to study and encourage them to learn what they missed. Instead of denigrating them for their failures, good teachers become "enablers" and use homework and testing as a way of helping them learn.

Macrorie describes "enablers," as educators whose primary approach is to help students do their best work. Macrorie says, "The teachers, or enablers,... work in startlingly similar ways and share many attitudes and principles. They all hold high expectations for learners. They arrange the learning place so that people draw fully on their present powers and begin to do good work. They support and encourage rather than punish. They ask learners to take chances that sometimes result in failure, and to use their mistakes productively" (Macrorie, *Twenty Teachers*, 229).

Someone has said that there is no such thing as failure—only data for reevaluating and improving performance. If a teacher emphasizes the fast failure and encourages students to be creative and to learn from their mistakes, everyone benefits. Teachers have more motivated students, and students learn at a faster, more satisfying pace.

11

Humor and the Enjoyment of Teaching

> "Humor is tragedy plus time."
> —Anonymous

STUDENTS IN A PHILOSOPHY-OF-RELIGION course at Butler University spent weeks studying intricate arguments for and against the existence of God. They looked at Anselm's arguments, Kant's critique of theism, and St. Thomas Aquinas's proofs for the existence of God. One day, the professor announced that the dreaded exam would be postponed. One student exclaimed, "There is a God" (*Readers Digest*, June 1988, 121–22).

Gilbert Highet notes that humor is one of the most important qualities of good teaching because it appeals to a strong human instinct—the love of play (Highet, *Art of Teaching*, 63). Humor has other advantages: it makes teaching more enjoyable and helps students learn better. Humor keeps their attention and contributes to the bonding essential to strong teacher-student relationships. A tribal dance goes on every time a teacher faces a new class of students. The teacher begins with some anxiety because she knows that each group is different and the chemistry between students and teacher can range from outstanding to negative.

First impressions in all relationships are important and teaching is no exception. From the moment she walks in, an instructor telegraphs to a class how she'll relate to them. If she comes off as stiff, arrogant and overly serious, students get jittery. Students are relieved if she projects the impression "I take learning seriously, but I like you and we can have fun in the process."

Joseph Lowman emphasizes that excellent teachers generate intellectual excitement and interpersonal rapport (*Mastering the Techniques of Teaching*, 13–18). Some teachers believe they can't combine the two. They reason that mixing warmth and learning will diminish the importance of the subject in students' eyes. For them, learning is sacred and you don't laugh in church.

But strong teachers have no problem fusing high academic standards with affection and a sense of fun. Humor and good teaching go together because laughter and play make learning more pleasant. The greater the pleasure, the more students are motivated to keep learning.

Humor has become serious business. American and Canadian industries have focused on humor as a way to increase productivity, diffuse tension and build overall morale. Teachers and students have been trading quips, puns, jokes and remarks for centuries, but lately, educators have focused on humor as a tool for better teaching. Civikly points out that humor in the classroom has at least two advantages: it increases attraction between both students and teacher, and it also relieves the anxiety which is part of any classroom (*Communicating in College Classrooms*, 64). Each of these results is well worth the effort to interject humor.

HUMOR: WHAT IS IT?

Most people recognize humor when they see or hear it, but humor is hard to define. E. B. White says, "Humor can be dissected, as a frog can, but the thing dies in the process and the innards are discouraging to any but the pure scientific mind" (Zinsser, *On Writing Well*, 190).

Humans are the only beings on earth who have a sense of humor. Dogs, cats and parakeets may provide mirth, but they don't have the power to laugh. Humor is closely linked to intelligence. Only humans can see the incongruous, make the connection between comedy and tragedy, and discern the sudden twist in the punch line.

Prolific author and avid joke collector Isaac Asimov (*Treasury of Humor*) maintains "that the one necessary ingredient in every successful joke is a sudden alteration in point of view." The quick twist and the unexpected contrast is the heart of humor. Patt Schwab, who gives advice on how to incorporate humor into speeches, tells the following story:

> A mother was having difficulty waking her son one morning. He pulled the covers over his head and told her, "I'm never going to school again. They hate me there. They make fun of me, and everybody talks about me behind my back." "Well," she said. "Get up. You are going to school, and you're going for two reasons. First,

you're forty-two years old, and second, you're the principal. So get up and get going."

Rodney Dangerfield once confessed: "I'm confused—but it's not my fault. Confusion is genetic. My father was confused. My grandfather was confused. In fact, my great grandfather was so confused that during the Civil War, he fought for the West."

Most students can remember instructors who were organized, held up high standards, communicated their ideas well, and also knew how to weave humor into their lectures or class discussions. Humor created a bond. Teachers with a sense of humor set a tone from the very beginning. Their humor might have been subtle, blatant, corny or a combination of all three, but they used it as a tool to teach.

Humor also relieves some of the anxiety that is part of most classrooms. Jean Civikly notes that "an undercurrent of tension is inherent in any close relationship and is released through joking" (*Communicating in College Classrooms*, 65). Classrooms can create tension because both teachers and students are on the spot to perform. Students are afraid of failure, and teachers often have the double challenge of trying to keep the lid on discipline and simultaneously get their material across. The quick quip at the right time is an escape valve and helps soften a volatile situation.

Humor helps the bonding process important to any relationship. People with a sense of humor are more attractive than those who are humorless. Students work harder for teachers they like and who make learning a joy instead of a grind. Eble emphasizes "Learning is enjoyable: it's especially enjoyable when there is a dose of humor attached to it" (*The Craft of Teaching*).

The teacher who knows how to use humor has a better chance to get and hold a student's attention. If a class knows that an instructor weaves humorous comments into lectures, they'll be more alert because they don't want to miss anything.

Mary Ann Glyn of Yale University found out that students who see problems as games arrive at more creative solutions than those who see the same problems as work ("All Work and No Play," 36). Alice Isen of the University of Maryland discovered that people who "felt good" after watching a funny film were also more creative in solving problems.

Humor is also a quick and effective way to get key points across in class. Zinsser points out that one Gary Trudeau Doonesbury comic strip "is worth a thousand words of moralizing." The books *Catch-22* or *Dr. Strangelove* are "more powerful than all the books and movies that try to show war 'as it is'" (Zinsser, *On Writing Well*, 184). The quick quip to illustrate a key point is often remembered longer than the point itself.

Students remember items that were funny and can recount them years later at class reunions. They forget in ten minutes what English king lost the battle of Hastings or what Portuguese explorer discovered Brazil. The trick is to link material in class to something funny so it stays in the mind longer than it would on its own.

HUMOR AND STRESS

Experts for centuries have touted the benefits of laughter. Over four hundred years ago, Robert Burton maintained that "Humor purges the blood, making the body young, lively and fit for any manner of employment" (Cousins, *Anatomy of an Illness*). Even Immanuel Kant, known more for his abstract philosophical theories than for his wit, says that "Humor is the feeling of health through the furtherance of the vital bodily process, the affection that moves the intestines and diaphragm: in a word, the feeling of health that makes up the gratification felt by us, so that we can reach the body through the soul and use the latter to realize the former" (ibid.).

Sigmund Freud believed that mirth was a useful way of counteracting nervous tension, and that laughter was effective therapy. More recently, William Fry of Stanford wrote a paper titled "The Respiratory Components of Mirthful Laughter." Fry emphasizes, "Humor helps the entire breathing process. Even when people go into uncontrollable laughter and say that their ribs hurt, they are relaxed almost to the point of an open sprawl."

Norman Cousins is well known for his contention that humor heals and reduces stress. In Anatomy of an Illness, Cousins recounts a time he was near death after returning from a trip to Europe. He admitted himself to a hospital and after a few days of needles, tubes and interruptions, checked out and tried an unusual approach for regaining his health. Cousins rented Three Stooges and Marx Brothers movies. He then sequestered himself in a hotel room for three days and watched the films. Laughter became his cure. In frequent lectures, Cousins promotes the advantages of humor. People who laugh fifteen times a day feel less stress than those who rarely laugh.

Professionals who work under pressure release catecolemones, described as tissue attackers. People who laugh often during the day release endorphins which heal the body and soothe the mind. If a teacher is tense and tired, a few laughs sprinkled throughout the day capped by watching a late-night comedy often work better than a tranquilizer.

Teaching on any level invites stress. An instructor in an inner city school who has to watch for knives and guns is under more pressure than a college teacher, but even college teachers can work under enormous tension. Despite movie images of the professor who leads a life of low-keyed tranquility, college teaching carries its own brand of stress, including requirements for promotion and tenure,

Teaching can, on occasion, numb the brain and wear down the body. Few teachers can escape the symptoms of stress, which include headaches, ulcers, high blood pressure, and an upset stomach. While humor is not a panacea for every malady resulting from stress, laughter is a teacher's good friend. The instructor who doesn't take herself too seriously, who makes an effort to blend laughter into her day, and who sees the incongruous side of classroom work will survive the hard parts of teaching.

Some instructors teach in a cauldron. Hostile students, explosive classrooms and too much work can try the most dedicated professionals. But other educators create their own stress because of the way they see the world. The slightest disruption throws them into a deep tailspin. Most experts on stress maintain that the outside event causing the stress is not as important as the individual's perception of it. One teacher can be devastated by mild criticism from a colleague, while another brushes it off. Each has the same experience, but each sees it differently. Perception shapes their reactions.

Humor is a way to diffuse such situations. For the teacher who has just been the target of criticism by a colleague, a sense of humor helps to put things in perspective. She says to herself "Okay, there's some merit to the comment that I didn't get my committee report in on time and thus inconvenienced four other people. I'll have to get myself in gear and make sure it doesn't happen again." Or if the criticism is unwarranted, she can say, "Hey look, I didn't deserve that blast. I can't help the other person's bad judgment and surly mood." Some things need to be taken seriously, but to look upon everything that happens during the school day as a major crisis is asking for frayed nerves and a gloom that turns a job into an ordeal.

HANDLE HUMOR WITH CARE

Humor is a two-edged sword. Used well, it can relieve tension, increase the teacher's effectiveness, and make learning experiences more pleasant. But when it backfires, humor can increase pressure, paint the instructor as a fool, and erode discipline. I like humor and try to sprinkle it into my classes. But many of my attempts over the years have bombed. One liners that seemed so funny on Jay Leno or David Letterman the night before have gone over with students like a lead blimp. Humor needs to be applied carefully to work well.

Jokes in particular are risky. If humor thrives on a sudden twist, the instructor is taking a big chance if he announces he wants to tell a new joke he just heard. As most joke tellers can attest, a joke that works is not merely the product of a good punch line but includes the right audience, occasion, and sense of timing. That's why most readers who buy arithologies of jokes are disappointed. Two or three jokes in the book may get a feeble smile from a reader, but without the context and timing, most published jokes are about as appetizing as last week's hors d'oeuvres. For example, take the following joke standing on its own:

> There was once a man named Murphy who walked by a mansion. On the front door was a sign that said, "Need painter. Will pay well." Murphy then knocked on the door and when the lady of the house appeared, Murphy said, "I'm a painter. I'll be glad to do the job for you." The woman replied, "I want my back porch painted green. Here's a brush and a bucket." Murphy picked up his tools and went to do the paint job. After a half hour, he appeared at the front door and said, "Your paint job is finished, ma'am." The woman responded, "How could you have painted the porch so fast." Murphy replied, "I'm a fast worker—and by the way, it's not a Porsche—it's a Mercedes."

Few readers would laugh at the preceding punch line as it appears in print. But take an Irish Rovers' concert, the atmosphere of merriment such concerts produce, and the proper telling by one of the Rovers, and the joke gets a big laugh.

Humor and the Enjoyment of Teaching

Most jokes standing alone are doomed to die. A joke or two deftly placed in a fifty question objective test or a funny story used to make a point can work, but it's risky to let jokes fly on their own.

INAPPROPRIATE HUMOR

The type of humor that almost always backfires is the putdown. Don Rickles made this genre his main form of comedy, and some teachers use derisive humor to keep students under control and to get a few laughs from the rest of the class. But humor that demeans inflicts more damage than it does good. A fine line exists between healthy kidding and the mean-spirited put-down. The high school sophomore who has been put in his place by a funny and caustic comment may laugh along with the rest of the class, but he's usually crying on the inside.

Successful humor in the classroom or anyplace else is hard. George Plimpton has played a number of roles and written books about them. In *The Paper Lion*, he tells about his experience of training with the Detroit Lions football team. But he says his hardest job was to try to be a stand-up comic in a nightclub. Despite having material from some of the best comedy writers, he still had flop sweat when he stood on-stage alone and a joke went down in flames.

SO, WHAT WORKS?

Humor in the classroom has the best chance of working when (1) it's appropriate to the instructor, (2) it fits the occasion, and (3) it is spontaneous. But spontaneity does not mean lack of planning. Effective humor comes across as fresh and seemingly unrehearsed, but most teachers who use it well have thought about ways to work it into their material. They don't make a joke or story stand on its own but use it to illustrate a point. For example, a teacher might want student participation. Therefore she could begin with the following story. There was once a man named Willard who went to the back of a church to pray. Willard said, "Lord I don't ask for much, but I would really appreciate your granting me just one small favor. Please help me win the state lottery." Willard left but came back a week later and went to one of the middle pews. This time he said, "Lord you say in Scripture that anything we ask for in prayer you will grant. I'm asking you again to please help me win the state lottery." Willard returned home and after the third week he came back, walked boldly to the front of the church and in a loud voice said, "Lord I have asked for this favor on two previous occasions. If you grant it, I promise that, in exchange, I'll recarpet the church and put in new stain glass windows. Please help me win the state lottery." There was a pause. Then a big voice came from the ceiling of the church and said, "Willard. You have to meet me halfway—buy a ticket."

The teacher might then tell the class that she would like them to "buy a ticket" by getting involved and contributing their share to class discussions. If the joke gets a laugh, that's fine. If it doesn't, that's all right too because the instructor was trying to make a point. A joke standing on its hind legs can fall flat. But one used to illustrate an idea will work if that is its main purpose.

CAN A TEACHER DEVELOP A BETTER SENSE OF HUMOR?

Some teachers are born comedians, but most funny people hone their comedic skills over a long period. Following are some methods that can help develop a sense of humor and apply it to teaching.

1. Be willing to risk. Much humor backfires and different students react to different kinds of humor. One may find a pun hilarious, and another thinks the teacher should never try anything funny again. Don't get discouraged. Most students appreciate the attempt at humor because it makes the teacher more approachable.

2. Be on the lookout for the incongruous. Collect anecdotes and put them in a file because memory slips away.. A good joke or story is gone 20 minutes after someone tells it.

3. Read the best comic writers you can. For outrageous humor, immerse yourself in Dave Barry. If you want more subtle wit, read E. B. White and Mark Twain. Erma Bombeck had a marvelous way of taking the ordinary and making it funny.

4. Watch comedians in action. Johnny Carson who was especially skilled at rescuing himself from a joke or situation that has bombed. Often, his deft escape was funnier than the original joke.

5. If you meditate, start the day by telling yourself that you'll see the humor in every out-of-sync situation. If things don't go the way

you plan, laugh at the incongruity. Because humor is often a way of perceiving, set your mind to see the off-beat.

6. Have a reader board with cartoons or funny messages. Many teachers do this for two reasons: (1) they show the world they can laugh, and (2) they provide a brief moment of respite for others. Cartoons from the *New Yorker* and Gary Larson's *The Far Side* go over well with most high-school and college students.

FINAL WORDS

Like anything else, humor is a matter of attitude. Two people can see the same event—a waiter dropping a tray of food on the lap of the school president—and respond in completely different ways. The president's secretary perceives the event as a disaster, and a colleague reacts with a burst of laughter. Just as a fine line separates tragedy from comedy, attitude means the difference between enjoying and enduring anything. Tragic events occur and laughter would be out of place. But much happens that is potentially funny. It would be a shame not to enjoy it.

If teaching is a joy for many, one of the major reasons for such satisfaction is the humor a classroom can provide. Most instructors who look back on the good times recall the laughter they shared with students and colleagues. On reflection, they also would agree that a sense of humor not only helped them get through the rough spots, but made them better teachers.

12

Making the Joy Last

> "God has given each of us the ability to do certain things well. If you are a teacher, do a good job of teaching."
>
> —St. Paul

In this book I have focused on the joys of teaching and have emphasized the connection between teaching well and finding satisfaction in the classroom. For myself and the teachers I interviewed, enjoyment has usually been the result of three factors: a love of students, a love of learning, and the ability to have a positive impact on students by helping them learn. On purpose I've acknowledged but downplayed the negative parts of teaching and concentrated on the positive.

Not every teacher makes education a life-time calling. Many leave after a time. They're attracted to teaching, stay in for a few years and then move on for a variety of reasons—better pay in another profession, disillusionment with a particular school system, or burn-out. But most of those who stay don't regret their decision, because teaching has given their life a deep sense of meaning. The ones who remain in the profession for a long time have some common ways of sustaining their satisfaction over the years.

Charles Van Riper is typical of teachers who have never regretted their choice of vocation. Van Riper taught speech pathology at Western Michigan University for forty years. One of his students was Ken Macrorie, who himself became a teacher at Western Michigan. Macrorie used to tell his students: "In this university works one of the great teachers in the world. If I were you, I wouldn't graduate until I had taken a class with him, no matter what my major field of study was."

Van Riper reflected on his teaching in an article for the Western Michigan student newspaper. Following is part of what he said: "I have just made the horrible discovery that I have taught the same undergraduate course, 'Introduction to Speech Pathology,' fifty-nine times and will teach it again next semester. The shudder is more of shock than revulsion. Incredibly, I contemplate this sixtieth performance, if that is what it is, with real enthusiasm. I like to teach that course!" (quoted in Macrorie, *Twenty Teachers*, 116).

Van Riper concludes his article with the following sentence: "And so I return to the hard fact that soon I shall teach 'Introduction to Speech Pathology' for the sixtieth time. Has all this been but the pumping of a tired balloon? Perhaps so, but I know that next fall semester when I walk into that amphitheatre, I shall hear the sound of trumpets" (ibid, 121).

How do teachers like Van Riper keep themselves going over the years and continue to enjoy what they do? What can a new teacher learn from someone who has been in the profession for a long time? Or what can a burnt-out instructor do to re-enkindle the fire? Following are some answers to those questions.

HAPPY TEACHERS LIKE THEIR STUDENTS

It may seem obvious that liking students is a prerequisite to liking education, but some teachers don't really like most of their students. They tolerate them because they have to. Once the class is over, they have little contact with them. Happy teachers, on the other hand, really like the students they encounter. Kathleen Lennon teaches fourth-graders in Frederick, Maryland. When you ask her where she gets her satisfaction, she responds like many other teachers: "The kids." Despite the long hours and hard work, Kathleen insists she wouldn't have any other job, because the students energize her.

Teaching is a people profession, and anyone who doesn't like students should find some other job. Most fulfilled educators talk about their interaction and the impact on those they've taught. They gain immense pleasure from seeing people advance, and relish knowing they have been part of the growing process. Charles Van Riper was a stutterer as a child and then went on to become an authority on the subject. Over many years he worked with stutterers and helped them gain control of their handicap. He turned a liability into an asset and was able to help hundreds of people who would have been disabled without his help.

Years after a class is over, ex-students call teachers and tell them how much they influenced them for good. Students send them cards at Christmas, give gifts out of the blue, and bring their children to meet someone who meant so much earlier in their life.

Parents call years after a daughter or son has gone through a particular class to tell a teacher that she had an immense impact. Comments range from "You were the one adult he trusted and respected" to "You have no idea how much good you did for my daughter when she was twelve because you cared."

An instructor who influences positively only one student in a lifetime knows that an entire teaching career is worth it. But effective teachers touch many lives in the course of an academic year. Knowing that a teacher has made a difference is a prime source of satisfaction. Teachers won't replace parents as the major influence in a child's life, but sometimes they can make a great difference. The best teachers illustrate Henry Adams's contention that "a teacher affects eternity; he can never tell where his influence stops."

FULFILLED TEACHERS KEEP ON LEARNING

Early Greeks like Plato and Epicurus emphasized that learning can be one of the highest forms of enjoyment, especially as one gets older. Physical pleasure may decline over the years but, like a fine wine, the joys of the intellect improve with age. Plato's system of study in the Academy was designed to cultivate the life of the mind. Some have called Plato a killjoy who wanted to spoil people's fun by suppressing the pleasures of the body. The philosopher from the fifth century B.C. was wise enough to know that bodily pleasures are intense at the time of enjoyment, but they fade fast. Intellectual joy, on the other hand, takes time to develop, but over the long haul provides more satisfying pleasure.

Most connoisseurs of classical music can remember that their first exposure to Bach, Beethoven and Mozart didn't excite them. But the more they listened, the better they enjoyed it. Children who read early come to savor the joys only a good book can bring.

By its very nature, education fosters learning. You can't teach a course unless you know its subject matter. One of the best ways to know something well is to have to teach it. Teaching demands an initial understanding of the subject followed by an organized presentation. I recall my own fuzzy grasp of philosophy—even though I had earned a licentiate degree in the subject. Then I was asked to teach an introductory course at a community college. I prepared hard for two months so I could clearly communicate abstract concepts to students who had never encountered Plato, Aristotle, Marx, or the Existentialists. Preparation made the material come alive, and I relished the challenge of taking a subject I had struggled to learn and getting a firm handle on it.

Most educators like to keep learning throughout their lives. Ruth Miller taught for over thirty-three years and found that her students always kept her challenged. She said, "I was intrigued by their responses to problems. They were always interesting and frequently surprising as they opened new possibilities for learning. After I retired, I spent ten years learning to paint. Watching students learn and learning myself has always been a joy."

Giovanni Costigan lived a full—if somewhat tumultuous—life. In an article citing his death at the age of 85, The *Seattle Post Intelligencer* described him as "the elfin historian whose giant intellect and powerful sense of justice touched generations of University of Washington students" (March 29, 1990, p. 1). Costigan championed liberal causes during his long teaching career and as a consequence incurred the wrath of some who didn't agree with his views. But his was a full life. He died while guest-lecturing on a cruise ship near Spain. Forced to retire after a forty-one-year career at the University, Costigan continued to teach classes through the Alumni Association. Even after retirement, he often drew 450 students to his courses.

Costigan always lived each day as if it were his last: "I feel time is very short. I'm always in a hurry. Not much time. Not much time at all. Therefore one must do what one can" (ibid).

A teacher who instills in students a love of learning has passed on a priceless gift. Learning in school is practical, because graduates can barter their knowledge for a better job and more money. But even if a student never applied what she learned in school to something practical, she would still have an investment that keeps nourishing her mind long after she first understood the material.

Few children are attracted by nature to the joys of thinking. But once exposed to the intricacy and solution of a math problem or Beethoven's Ninth Symphony, a select few start to realize that joys of the mind last longer and are far more fulfilling than those of the body. Teachers are often the conveyors of such a joy. Their own enthusiasm for history, literature, politics or religion is infectious.

SUSTAINING JOY BY TEACHING WELL

Quality is often its own reward. The happiest teachers are usually good at what they do. Most people who excel in a profession are far more fulfilled than those who are mediocre or inept. Just as a cabinetmaker gains great pleasure in making a piece of flawless furniture and selling it with pride to a customer, a teacher finds satisfaction in teaching well. Lowman notes: "Instructors should . . . aim for excellent classroom teaching because it is more rewarding to try to do anything well than to accept mediocrity" (*Mastering the Techniques of Teaching*). My brother Dick taught English at a high school in Portland, Oregon, and had a reputation as a popular but demanding teacher. He has enjoyed teaching for the past nineteen years because "it's always interesting and keeps me young. I also get pleasure from making a difference in someone's life. When college students I've had come back to visit, I always ask them, 'Did we miss anything? Did you feel prepared when you started your college English classes?' Their affirmative response gives me the satisfaction that what I did paid off."

An educational system is only as good as the professionals who teach in the classrooms. Good teachers will continue to be the sine qua non of quality education. A skilled teacher can conduct classes in a one-room country schoolhouse with borrowed texts, pencils, and notepads and make a class first-rate. An ineffective instructor can have the best audiovisuals, the latest equipment, plus the newest building and still make a class flounder. Computers can help teach, but they can never replace dedicated instructors who know their subject matter well, can explain that subject matter to their students, and like what they are doing.

For most of the teachers I interviewed and for the others I read about, quality meant knowing their subject matter well and transmitting it with clarity and enthusiasm. Such knowledge and skill often came from a concentrated program to improve teaching. Some teachers spend their summers learning more about their discipline while others attended workshops to improve their pedagogical methods. Few of the best teachers were satisfied that they had finally mastered either their subject or the art of teaching. They worked hard to get better over the years.

Making the Joy Last

A committee of professors and administrators at Miami-Dade College drew up (and published in *The Chronicle of Higher Education*, April 13, 1988) the following list of "core of fundamental characteristics" that describe excellent faculty members. Excellent faculty members:

1. Are enthusiastic about their work
2. Set challenging performance goals for themselves
3. Set challenging performance goals for students
4. Are committed to education as a profession
5. Project a positive attitude about students' ability to learn
6. Display behavior consistent with professional standards
7. See students as individuals operating in a broader perspective beyond the classroom
8. Treat students with respect
9. Are available to students
10. Listen attentively to what students say
11. Are responsive to student needs
12. Give corrective feedback promptly to students
13. Are fair in their evaluations of student progress
14. Present ideas clearly
15. Respect diverse talents
16. Create a climate conducive to learning
17. Work collaboratively with colleagues
18. Are knowledgeable about their work
19. Provide perspectives that include a respect for diverse views
20. Do their work in a well-prepared manner
21. Do their work in a well-organized manner
22. Are knowledgeable about how students learn
23. Provide students with alternative ways of learning
24. Stimulate intellectual curiosity
25. Encourage independent thinking

26. Provide cooperative learning opportunities for students
27. Encourage students to be analytical listeners
28. Give consideration to feedback from students and others
29. Provide clear and substantial evidence that students have learned.

    Joseph Lowman underscores other qualities that make teaching highly rewarding: an ability to captivate a student audience for an hour or more, to stimulate students intellectually and emotionally, to instill a love for the subject taught and a desire to learn more about it and to move students to work on their own (ibid).

    Master teachers reflect a number of skills. Their lecture or lesson is well organized and full of variety. They glide from abstract principles to informative anecdotes. They use their voices as a precision instrument to soothe, shout, whisper or prod. They weave into their presentations intriguing examples from newspapers, novels or short stories but always with the purpose of better explaining material. They know their subject well but are always looking for new ways to put it across. When they talk, their eyes light on one student for a short time and move on until they make eye contact with another. They telegraph the message that they care deeply about their students and their subject matter. They never stop learning themselves and they keep polishing their teaching skills over the years.

    The best and most fulfilled teachers are the opposite of those who teach poorly. A hypothetical composite of a poor teacher would include the following: the teacher speaks in a monotone, often reads from the text, and resents questions from students because they interrupt the planned lesson. In presenting material, the teacher hovers in the clouds of abstraction rather than the lowlands of specific examples and human interest anecdotes to reinforce ideas. The instructor rarely establishes eye contact but prefers to gaze at a spot five feet above the head of a student in the last row. Such teachers relay the message nonverbally that they'd rather be doing something else than teaching, but they have to make a living. They are part of the reason for the cliché: "Those who can, do. Those who can't, teach."

    Besides interviewing numerous teachers about what makes their profession satisfying, I also asked students what they liked about their best teachers. Individual answers varied, but the patterns were the same. Most verified Lowman's assessment of strong teachers as the ones who liked their students and had a lasting influence on them. Such instructors took time to learn names quickly and sent the message "I care about you and want you to gain as much as you can from my class during the time we're together." They usually stayed in touch after a class was over.

Students often rated their demanding teachers the best because they set high standards and insisted their charges live up to those standards. Students gave high marks to the combination of caring and intellectual rigor. Some could recall instructors who were well organized, knowledgeable about their subject and skilled in communicating, but who were cold and distant. Students said they learned, but weren't as motivated to learn as they were by someone who was both demanding and who cared about them as people. Other students talked about teachers who were affable but who didn't teach them much.

VARIETY HELPS MAINTAIN THE JOY

Strong teachers keep themselves stimulated by often trying something new in their courses or in their professional life. Peter Beidler was the Council for Advancement and Support of Education Professor of the Year in 1983. In an article entitled "The Joys of College Teaching," Beidler shares the reasons for his success and satisfaction. He admits that teaching can be boring and full of problems unless the teacher is creative.

Beidler does something different every term. He says: "One of the life-saving discoveries I have made about teaching is that my job as a teacher is not to discover what works in a classroom and then to spend the rest of my life making it work again and again ('The Joys of College Teaching'). That way lies boredom for me and my students. No, my job is to keep searching for ways to make my job fresh each term."

Beidler took his students to Arizona for a week to study Hopi Indians and write about their experiences. Another time, he and his students went to a bee farm. He said, "Taking my freshmen students to a bee farm may sound like a dumb idea, but we ... all learned something out there—about bees, about each other, about ourselves, about writing, about teaching."

Some instructors find joy by changing their teaching environment. Henriette Klauser taught for a number of years at the university level but then found she liked the stimulation of teaching writing to adults in workshops. In her lectures to business professionals, fellow educators, or writers, Henriette doles out doses of wit, warmth, and wisdom as she helps people get over their fear of writing. She exudes a confidence born of careful preparation. She's a teacher who gains immense joy from doing something well and sharing it with others. From her well-organized sessions to the viewgraphs she shows to actively involving her audience, she reflects the strong link between liking what one does and quality education.

Satisfied teachers rarely do the same thing year after year. If college teachers have a sabbatical available to them, they take it. During the semester or year away from their regular teaching duties, they might work on a scholarly project or travel to Mexico. Sometimes a combination of work and recreation gives them the lift they need to go back to the classroom rejuvenated.

Many primary and secondary teachers use the summer to get more education or to do something different. Like the sabbatical, the three month summer break helps teachers get a change of scenery. Even educators who choose to teach during the summer months often offer a class different from the ones they teach during the academic year.

ENJOYMENT THROUGH SELF-ACTUALIZATION

Marsha Sinetar is an educator and organizational psychologist who conducted a survey on self-actualization. She describes individuals who live a simple outward life-style but who enjoy a rich interior life (*Do What You Love*). Such people see their work not as a job to get a paycheck, but as a vocation that allows them to fulfill one of their deepest needs. Dedicated and skilled teachers fit that pattern. Most teachers know they could make' more money in another job. They continue in the classroom because they really like what they do. They believe they're making a difference.

One of the teachers in Sinetar's study taught for the "joy of seeing kids learn. I teach in the trust that there is a future for humanity. My work is play. It is self-expression. It gives meaning, structure, and purpose to my whole life" (ibid.).

Sinetar found a three-part pattern to self-actualized people. First, they recognize they have unique talents and want to share what they have with others. Second, such sharing provides "a kinship, or sense of relatedness, to others. Third, this kinship produces a strong love that is constantly manifested in their thoughts and activities. Humans feel best when they are giving. When they can combine the twin needs of affection and self-actualization, they gain a deep sense of meaning.

One of the teachers who participated in Marsha Sinetar's study said, "If you've read *Goodbye Mr. Chips*, then you know how I feel about my work. For me teaching is a way of developing family—not in the personalized way most people think of, but as Mr. Chips said in the final pages of the book. When someone said to him that it was too bad he didn't have children of his own, he answered, 'It's wrong to think I've had no children. I've had hundreds and hundreds of children.' And that's exactly how I feel" (ibid., 66).

Sinetar demonstrates a link between success and self-esteem. In answering the question of how confident people can have an advantage over others less confident, she says, "The answer is found partially in their idea of self—their verdict about their likeability, their competence, their "powerfulness" or ability to handle life." In other words, the answer rests in your self-esteem. People who like themselves allow themselves to succeed in all aspects of life—even in their work) Teachers with high self-esteem usually make their students feel good about themselves. Confident students, in turn, learn better. Psychologist Sol Gordon maintains that the two best ways to raise self-esteem and reduce depression are to learn something new and to work for the good of others. Teaching provides the climate for both activities. Excellent educators keep learning, and they benefit their students by helping them develop their potential. Teaching has the advantage of allowing its practitioners to stay self-actualized over a long time. Most people can look at brief parts of their life when everything came together—good job, right family situation and the opportunity to use one's talents. But the time of self-actualization was short because the job changed or they became bored with what they were doing. Good teachers keep learning and continue to exert a positive influence on their students. These two pleasures never get old, and this helps account for teaching as a profession that yields such rich rewards.

Well over half of people who work don't like what they do. They hold a job because they have to put food on the table and pay the rent. But they don't bound out of bed in the morning happily anticipating a day at work. A small number of others have found the secret that work that matches talent and disposition with serving others means the difference between a life of drudgery and great satisfaction.

Most happy teachers see what they do as a vocation rather than a way to earn a paycheck. The Latin word *vocare* means "to call." Fulfilled and effective teachers believe strongly they have been given certain gifts that they want to use in the service of others. Many believe that God gives such gifts for a specific purpose. Having received such a gift, they develop and make it multiply. Like the man in the gospel who took what his master had given him and multiplied it four times, quality teachers continue to hone their own skills. With an effectiveness born of hard work and a quiet confidence in their abilities, fulfilled teachers enjoy what they do and keep getting better over the years. Like Charles Van Riper, they hear the sound of trumpets each time they start a new class.

Teaching doesn't make educators rich but produces a joy money could never buy for those who do it well. Such educators believe they have the best job in the world.

Bibliography

Asimov, Isaac. *Treasury of Humor: A Lifetime Collection of Favorite Jokes, Anecdotes, and Limericks with Copious Notes on How to Tell Them and Why*. Boston: Houghton Mifflin, 1971.
Baird, James, editor. *Course Critique*. Seattle: Associated Students, University of Washington, 1965.
Beidler, Peter G. "The Joys of College Teaching." *National Forum: Phi Kappa Phi Journal* 67.1 (1987) 3–6.
Bloom, Allan David. *The Closing of the American Mind: How Higher Education has Failed Democracy and Impoverished the Souls of Today's Students*. New York: Simon & Schuster, 1987.

Calkins, Lucy McCormick. *The Art of Teaching Writing*. Portsmouth, NH: Heinemann, 1986.
Cheney, Theodore A. Rees. *Getting the Words Right: 39 Ways to Improve Your Writing*. 2nd ed. Cincinnati: Writer's Digest Books, 2005.
Cialdini, Robert B. *Influence: Science and Practice*. 2nd ed. Glenview, IL: Scott, Foresman, 1988.
Civikly, Jean M. *Communicating in College Classrooms*. New Directions for Teaching and Learning 26. San Francisco: Jossey-Bass, 1986.
Conklin, Robert. *How to Get People to Do Things*. New York: Ballantine, 1982.
Cousins, Norman. *Anatomy of an Illness as Perceived by the Patient: Reflections on Healing and Regeneration*. New York: Norton, 1979.
Eble, Kenneth Eugene. *The Craft of Teaching: A Guide to Mastering the Professor's Art*. 2nd ed. San Francisco: Jossey-Bass, 1988.
Frankl, Viktor E. *Man's Search for Meaning: An Introduction to Logotherapy*. 3rd ed. New York: Simon & Schuster, 1984.
Franklin, Jon. *Writing for Story: Craft Secrets of Dramatic Nonfiction by a Two-Time Pulitzer Prize Winner*. New York: Atheneum, 1986.
Gallway, Paul. "Top Teachers Learn Lessons." *Spokesman Review*, 1989, sec. A.
Ginott, Haim G. *Teacher and Child; A Book for Parents and Teachers*. New York: Macmillan, 1972.
Glyn, Mary Ann. "All Work and No Play Isn't Even Good for Work." *Psychology Today*, March 1989, 34–38. Online: http://www.csc-scc.gc.ca/text/pblct/forum/e011/e011j-eng.shtml/.
Goldhaber, Gerald M. *Organizational Communication*. 4th ed. Dubuque, IA: Brown, 1986.
Hanna, Michael S., and James W. Gibson. *Public Speaking for Personal Success*. Dubuque, IA: Brown, 1987.

Bibliography

Hayakawa, S. I. *Language in Thought and Action.* 2nd ed. New York: Harcourt, Brace & World, 1964.

Heller, Scott. "Miami-Dade College Begins Project to Bolster Teaching by Evaluating New Professors and Rewarding Classroom Performance." *The Chronicle of Higher Education* 34.31 (April 13, 1988) A12–A18.

Highet, Gilbert. *The Art of Teaching.* New York: Knopf, 1950.

Howard, V. A., and J. H. Barton. *Thinking on Paper.* New York: Morrow, 1986.

Kasulis, Thomas P. "Questioning." In *The Art and Craft of Teaching,* edited by Margaret Morganroth Gullette, 38–48. Cambridge: Harvard University Press, 1982.

Kidder, Tracy. *Among Schoolchildren.* Franklin Center, PA: Franklin Library, 1989.

Klauser, Henriette Anne. *Writing on Both Sides of the Brain: Breakthrough Techniques for People Who Write.* San Francisco: Perennial Library, 1987.

Kushner, Harold S. *When All You've Ever Wanted Isn't Enough.* New York: Summit, 1986.

Lakein, Alan. *How to Get Control of Your Time and Your Life.* New York: Signet, 1974.

Lauerman, Connie. "Teachers Can't Tell Good Prose from Bad." *Chicago Tribune,* November 30, 1975.

Lederer, Richard. "Of Alices and Humpty Dumptys." *Writer's Digest* 69.3 (March 1989) 8.

Lowman, Joseph. *Mastering the Techniques of Teaching.* San Francisco: Jossey-Bass, 1984.

Mackenzie, R. Alec. *The Time Trap: How to Get More Done in Less Time.* New York: McGraw-Hill, 1975.

Macrorie, Ken. *Twenty Teachers.* New York: Oxford University Press, 1984.

McKeachie, Wilbert James. *Teaching Tips: A Guidebook for the Beginning College Teacher.* 8th ed. Lexington, MA: Heath, 1986.

McMillan, James H. *Assessing Students' Learning.* New Directions for Teaching and Learning 34. San Francisco: Jossey-Bass, 1988.

Nichols, Ralph G., and Leonard A. Stevens. *Are You Listening?* New York: McGraw-Hill, 1957.

Patent, Arnold M. *You Can Have It All.* Sylva, NC: Celebration, 1991.

Peck, M. Scott. *The Road Less Traveled: A New Psychology of Love, Traditional Values, and Spiritual Growth.* New York: Simon & Schuster, 1978.

Peters, Thomas J. *Thriving on Chaos: Handbook for a Management Revolution.* New York: Knopf, 1987.

Plimpton, George. *The Paper Lion.* New York: Perennial Library 1988.

Powell, John. *Why Am I Afraid to Tell You Who I Am?* London: Fontana, 1975.

Raphael, Ray. *The Teacher's Voice: A Sense of Who We Are.* Portsmouth, NH: Heinemann, 1985.

Sanfield, Steve. *Could This Be Paradise?: Tales of Sages from the Jewish Tradition.* Audiocassette. North San Juan, CA: North Backlog Book Services, 1987.

Sarnoff, Dorothy. *Speech Can Change Your Life: Tips on Speech, Conservation, and Speechmaking.* New York: Dell, 1972.

Siegel, Bernie S. *Love, Medicine & Miracles: Lessons Learned about Self-Healing from a Surgeon's Experience with Exceptional Patients.* New York: Harper & Row, 1986.

Simons, Herbert W. *Persuasion: Understanding, Practice, and Analysis.* 2nd ed. New York: Random House, 1976.

Sinetar, Marsha. *Do what You Love, the Money Will Follow: Discovering Your Right Livelihood.* New York: Paulist, 1987.

———. *Ordinary People as Monks and Mystics: Lifestyles for Self-Discovery.* New York: Paulist, 1986.

Bibliography

Smith, L. Glenn, Joan K. Smith, and F. Michael Perko. *Lives in Education: A Narrative of People and Ideas*. 2nd ed. New York: St. Martin's, 1994.

Strunk, William Jr., and E. B. White. *The Elements of Style*. 3rd ed. New York: Macmillan, 1979.

Sykes, Charles J. *ProfScam: Professors and the Demise of Higher Education*. Washington DC: Regnery Gateway, 1988.

Turner, Paul. "Will Meeters Ever Prosper?" *Spokesman Review*, October 13, 1988, sec. C 1, 6.

Weimer, Maryellen. *The Teaching Professor*.

Wilbert, Deborah. "The Right Way." *Spokesman Review*, April 26, 1989, sec. C1.

Williams, Redford B. *The Trusting Heart: Great News About Type A Behavior*. New York: Times Books, 1989.

Zinsser, William Knowlton. *On Writing Well: An Informal Guide to Writing Nonfiction*. 5th ed. New York: HarperPerennial, 1994.

www.ingramcontent.com/pod-product-compliance
Lightning Source LLC
Chambersburg PA
CBHW070911160426
43193CB00011B/1422